» SAYING YES «
TO LIFE

‹» SAYING YES «
TO LIFE
As We Grow Older ›

JOSEPHINE ROBERTSON

Nashville   Abingdon Press   New York

SAYING YES TO LIFE

Copyright © 1965, 1966 by Abingdon Press

Library of Congress Catalog Card Number: 66-21191

"The Lord's Garden" is reprinted by permission of Guideposts. The quotation from Yankee from Olympus, by
Catherine Drinker Bowen, is used by permission of Little,
Brown and Company, Publishers. The quotation on pp.
16-17 was originally published in Friends Journal and
is used by permission. The quotations on pp. 7, 14, and
15 are reprinted by permission of Alfred A. Knopf, Inc.
from Markings by Dag Hammarskjöld, trans. by Leif
Sjoberg and W. H. Auden. Copyright © 1964 by Alfred
A. Knopf, Inc. and Faber & Faber, Ltd. The quotation
from Dear Gift of Life is used by permission of Pendle
Hill Publications.

SET UP, PRINTED, AND BOUND BY THE
PARTHENON PRESS, AT NASHVILLE,
TENNESSEE, UNITED STATES OF AMERICA

Dedicated to
Philip and David
who have enriched our lives

Chapter 10

Pitch and Octave

FOREWORD

You dare your Yes—and experience a meaning.
You repeat your Yes—and all things acquire a meaning.
When everything has a meaning, how can you live anything but a *Yes?*

—Dag Hammarskjöld

There are many ways of saying Yes to life, and these become more important as the years advance. When we say Yes, a door opens. We need open doors in our later years, doors that open on people of all ages, on books, nature, service, the inspiration of Christ, and the sustaining relationship with God. With such an outlook, in time of illness or sorrow we will not waste our strength on the torturing question, "Why did this happen to me?" We will accept

7

what comes as the farmer accepts hail, drought, and frost. The question is not "Why?" but "How do I deal with this?" There are many circumstances over which we have no control, but the response is of our own making.

In these pages I tell of men and women who have lived a Yes in meeting the problems of later life and learned, with serenity, to say Yes to the end of life as we know it. It is my hope that their stories may open the doors for others on a richer, more meaningful experience.

I should like to express appreciation to the many friends who have been helpful in the preparation of this book. The list, which is not complete, includes Mr. and Mrs. Robert S. Craig, Miss Esther C. Stammats, Mrs. Dora C. Davis, Mrs. Ralph Patterson, and the Rev. J. Earl Cummings. A very special word of thanks goes to the Rev. Paul L. Denise and the Rev. C. Luther Fulmer, Jr.

JOSEPHINE ROBERTSON

CONTENTS

» 1. Finding Meaning in Life «

I will sing unto the Lord as long as I live: I will sing praise to my God while I have my being.

—Psalm 104:33

He was one of the most important men in the world. The fate of nations was affected by his wisdom and skill. He was a quiet man, held in honor by millions who thought he fitted easily into his role with a cool, untroubled brilliance. After his sudden death the world learned otherwise, for Dag Hammarskjöld, Secretary-General of the United Nations from 1953 to 1961, chose to share with mankind the secret behind his calm and handsome presence. From his journal we know now that this great man, tortured by doubt, foreboding, and loneliness, found his sustaining strength in a powerful religious faith. Few had suspected the depth of a spiritual inner life which led him to regard the strains and dangers of his post as an opportunity given him by God. Dag Hammarskjöld, a complex and gifted man, died in his effort to achieve peace. His life was sacrificed for this goal and was a sacrifice which he had felt awaited him.

His journal, *Markings*, is not a diary in the usual

sense as it names no names, describes no historical events. Rather, it records in beautiful fragments of prose and poetry, the writer's spiritual groping and inspiration. The meaning of the title is clearer when one understands that the English title is used to translate the Norwegian *Vägmärken,* a term which refers to the guideposts or markers along a trail. The entries in this record mark the trail of a noble soul. Perhaps the most telling entry is this:

I don't know Who—or what—put the question, I don't know when it was put. I don't even remember answering. But at some moment I did answer *Yes* to Someone—or Something—and from that hour I was certain that existence is meaningful and that, therefore, my life, in self-surrender, had a goal.

He refers in several places to the thought of saying Yes to life and to sacrifice, but there are other concepts helpful to men and women searching for meaning through trials and hardships in the years of maturity.

"We are not permitted," he writes, "to choose the frame of our destiny. But what we put into it is ours."

Looking backward, we see there are indeed many

who would prefer a different frame for their destiny, different circumstances of birth, family, opportunity, physical endowment. Perhaps bright hopes for success and loving relationships were wiped out by tragedy. There are many factors in every life beyond the control of the individual, and yet there are many ways of living with these limiting factors.

This thought can become increasingly relevant as we grow older. We think of our mature friends and members of our families. Some, resenting age, grow moody and self-centered. Others, transcending handicaps, have a kind of radiance. These have said Yes to life, with all its pain, adventure, and joy. Their days have meaning, and they use them well. While few are called to greatness, many live lives great in spirit. We appreciate their example, as we appreciate the trail markings left for us by Dag Hammarskjöld. Whatever our age we can share his beautiful prayer:

Give me a pure heart—that I may see Thee,
A humble heart—that I may hear Thee,
A heart of love—that I may serve Thee,
A heart of faith—that I may abide in Thee.

» 2. Remembering the Way It Was «

Neither do men light a candle, and put it under a bushel, but on a candlestick; and it giveth light unto all that are in the house.

—Matthew 5:15

Some people have the ability to sense and meet another's need.

When the boy reached the platform in the Friends' conference hall, he was swept with terror. Not a word would come to his lips, not a thought to his panic-stricken mind. The silence was painful, as he stood there, and the audience suffered with him. Suddenly an elderly gentleman arose from his seat near the front of the hall and looked at the boy with kindness.

"What is thy name?"

He murmured the words, almost inaudibly.

"Where is thy home?"

"Philadelphia."

"And how old is thee?"

"Fourteen." The voice was a little stronger.

"What group has thee been attending?"

"Junior High."

"What has thee come to tell us?"

16

With this the panic evaporated, and the boy launched into a good report. At the end he turned to his rescuer and said, "Thank you." This was an experience of understanding which would not be forgotten, by any who had shared his ordeal.

What might inspire a man to such unusual action? Probably a rule of kindness, which had governed his life, but also a sympathetic memory of what it was like to be young and unsure. We can be sure the thought never entered the elderly Friend's mind that his action might be a candle to give light to "all that are in the house."

The gift of fresh, intuitive understanding, is one which glows ever more brightly from the polish of use.

If we tend, for example, to be critical of our neighbor's children, it helps to think back to how it was with our children and then distil our own experience into helpfulness. When our children have homes of their own and we do not think they are wise about finance, about planning, about family activities, it helps to remember ourselves at that age. Were we so wise about everything? We learned not so much from our elders as through our own mistakes and experience.

"Should I interfere and tell them what I think they should do?" a troubled mother asks.

"No," says the father thoughtfully. "They are adults now. Praise them for the things they do well and take every opportunity to show your faith in them. They will learn."

We are impressed, as we read of Christ's personal encounters with the people of his day, by the skill with which he could penetrate their thinking and the way he could understand their problems. They felt they were talking to someone who really understood and to whom their concerns were important. We, too, can learn to be understanding and perceptive. Often we can encourage others with insight based on troubled experiences of the past. It is a privilege to be able to say, "Yest, I know just how you feel, but I know there is a way."

Our Father, help us not only to sense another's need, but to answer it with the wisdom of experience and the inspiration of thy love.

» 3. A Flower in the Buttonhole «

The glory of young men is their strength: and the beauty of old men is the gray head.

—Proverbs 20:29

When I read this verse I think of a gentleman who was in his eighties when we came to know him through a literary society, of which he had been a member for forty years. He was light of build and there was beauty, not only in his silvery gray hair, but in his face and in his spirit. "A man's wisdom makes his face to shine," according to Ecclesiastes 8:1, and this was true of our friend. He took great care of his appearance and often had a flower in his buttonhole. Although extremely deaf, he was interested in the members of the group and always had a courteous personal remark or query for each. He was well acquainted with the classics under discussion, whether Shakespeare, Gibbon, or Tolstoy, and, if he dozed during the papers, of which he could catch little even with his hearing aid, he always had some contribution, based on his reading, to enrich the later discussion.

Life was meaningful to him until the end. Long a widower, he maintained his fine old house by advertising for a young couple willing to exchange generous living space and meals for simple housekeeping. A succession of couples, starting on professional or scientific careers, lived with him, and a number of babies were born during their residencies. Some of the brides were not very good cooks, but he was too philosophical to complain and enjoyed the young life around him.

We like to think of our friend, now gone peacefully to rest, because he revealed how gracious age can be. We remember how well turned out he looked, for, in the later years, care of appearance indicates not only a sense of personal dignity, but a consideration for others. Careful dressing and grooming involve more effort with age, but hold values, both for the individual and his associates.

When we are young, we enjoy looking our best, both from natural pride and to make a good impression, usually on the opposite sex. This adds to our confidence, gives us more poise and releases our thoughts from ourselves, allowing us to concentrate on others. Any woman who has been in the hospital knows the wonderful boost in morale that comes the first time she can have her hair "done" and put on something pretty. Looking back to our childhood, we realize that there was psychology, as well as soap and starch, in our Sunday best.

Furthermore, unless we are beatniks, we like to be with people who look attractive. Recently I saw a ninety-six-year-old woman emerging from the beauty parlor of a home for the aged, her hair nicely waved. She took pride in being a creditable part of her group.

Children like to see their mothers and their teachers look pretty. A little later the girls like well-dressed escorts, and the boys want to be proud of the girls' appearance. Husbands appreciate wives who look trim, even at breakfast, and so it goes all through life. We take it as a compliment when our companions are careful of their appearance, and we enjoy their company more because of their thoughtfulness.

Character, strong and warm, can create a special kind of beauty in faces long past youth. There is, indeed, beauty in gray hair—especially when it is well combed!

Our Father, strengthen our self-respect and may the outward signs show inner faith in thy purpose for our lives.

» 4. Other Things to Do Now «

A good man out of the good treasure of his heart bringeth forth that which is good. —Luke 6:45

The elderly minister spoke reflectively and just a bit wistfully.

"This is the first time in forty-four years that I have not preached on Mother's Day. Yes, I miss the pulpit, but I figure there are other things for me to do now."

Indeed there were, for this man had sparked the building of a church retirement home and now, with his physical activities limited, was available there for counseling when any of the residents sought help with personal problems.

The step from pulpit to pew can be a long one, but this kindly man was facing forward with the faith that there were other opportunities ahead.

What are these "other things"? This is the question that confronts men and women who come, often reluctantly, to the end of the well-marked highway of job, homemaking, or career. Little roads go off in all directions. Do they fade into useless paths? Are they dead ends? Do they lead to desirable destinations? The trail markings are few and not specific at this point in the journey, and it may be necessary to try several before finding the best road.

For a time freedom to wander may be exhilarating, as with children at the start of a long vacation. Then may come that familiar question, "But what shall I do *now?*"

Each of us has some special skill or dexterity developed through the years, in homemaking, the arts, crafts, business, mechanics, teaching, or dealing with people. Although many engage in post-retirement jobs, most of us do not expect to embark on major new careers. We find satisfaction, however, by using, in some fashion, our special abilities.

As the mother of a friend expressed it, "It's not just a matter of what shall I do? There are plenty of ways to put in time. The important question is 'What can I do to be useful?' I have found this the key to happiness."

An excellent homemaker, she offered to keep house for a sister who was very busy giving music lessons. The arrangement has worked out happily. She enjoys the children who visit her sister at the piano and finds that today's apparently sophisticated youth have the same appetite for cookies as those that came before.

A kindergarten teacher celebrated her retirement with a round of trips and visits. After a while she began to feel a lack and volunteered to spend some of her mornings teaching a preschool group at a settlement house.

A former engineer in a retirement community discovered a constant need of repairs in the homes of his neighbors. He went into business, charging nominal fees in order that people would feel free to call him. Earnings are small, but he enjoys the use of his tools, helping people, and making new friends.

With our own seeking, and God's guidance, we can find an arrow which points to those *other useful things.*

Guide us, we pray, into absorbing activities which will serve others and so serve thee.

» 5. Moving «

The Lord shall preserve thy going out and thy coming in from this time forth, and even for evermore.

—Psalm 121:8

Our house was empty. The moving van had rumbled ahead of us down the road, as we drove out of our gate for the last time. There was a lump in my throat as my husband paused to take our name off the mailbox, an action that marked the finality of many rich years in this place. Sensing my feeling, he said quietly, "You know, this is the *beginning* of a new chapter."

There are many changes in modern living, and, if we say Yes to life, we regard them not as ends but as beginnings.

Some of our friends have been transferred a dozen times. Hardly are the curtains up in a new house when the call comes to an assignment in another city. Plans must be cancelled, school activities interrupted, a house must be sold, a new house, church, school, doctors, dentists, and new friends must be found—and, in the interval, that strange feeling of belonging nowhere.

It happens frequently that a parent or parents

move to a completely strange community to be close to their children, only to have the children whisked hundreds of miles away. In former times our ancestors usually lived out their years in one place, often never traveling more than a few miles. Do today's nomads suffer from the lack of such stability? Not necessarily. Experience has shown that physical stability is not as important as emotional security.

When hundreds of children of migrant construction workers moved into our community a few years ago, the superintendent of schools told me that, not only did these trailer-dwelling children offer few problems, but that they enriched the experience of the classes through their cross-country travels. The mothers of families that move often tell me that close family ties and a strong church relationship are most helpful, because both give the strength of belonging. The children learn to make new friends. They learn to volunteer and participate in church and school activities without waiting on the sidelines to be sought out.

Nevertheless, uprooting is never easy, whether for the child who misses a special playmate, the mother who must build a home over again, or the retiree who is lonely for old friends, the roses of a special garden, or the pastor whose sermons seemed to speak directly to one's needs. But it may be that along with today's mobile children we have a truer perspective on life than those who could count on the permanence of their environment— and whose homes were not in danger of being swept away for a highway cloverleaf.

Stability today must lie in intangible values. Those who move learn that there are different ways of life, kinds of people, modes of worship, but that love of God, family affection, integrity, and the way of the good neighbor underlie Christian living wherever they may be.

As each chapter ends, we will not say "this is the end," but "this is a beginning." Treasuring the rich experience of the past, we will look forward with faith to what lies ahead.

Help us, our Father, to find opportunity in change and courage for new chapters of our lives.

» 6. "I'm Never Lonely" «

A man that hath friends must shew himself friendly.

—Proverbs 18:24

When I hear discussion of the forlorn and common problem of loneliness, I like to think of a delightful person I met while we were both working on a YWCA project. She was so lively and friendly that one liked her at once, for we are all drawn to those who live with zest. Yet her life had not been easy. Her husband had died while he was still a young man, and she had worked hard, making her own way and educating their child. Now that she had reached retirement age she had come across the continent and had recently taken an apartment a few miles from her daughter's home.

"Do you find it lonely in a strange city?" I asked.

"Lonely? I'm never lonely—and I've been alone a great deal. Last year I took a room in a women's hotel in New York City for several months. Didn't know a soul when I went."

"How did you make out? I've known some women who found life alone in a strange city so miserable it was almost frightening."

"I had a wonderful time! Sometimes I would

28

spend a whole day at the Metropolitan Museum. I took a course of free sewing lessons at a big department store. Sundays I often went to two different churches, and anyone who says they don't care about strangers in city churches is all wrong. I didn't try to go out much at night, but found some nice people at the hotel. When I'm alone I like to read or sew."

"Naturally it's different here because you have your family."

"Yes, I enjoy them very much, but I'm only with them part of the time. I've found some courses here at the YW that I've always wanted to take, and I've offered to help wherever they need me. They find a lot for me to do. Another thing I like to do that doesn't cost much is to take bus trips and see the country. Next year I'm planning to give up my apartment and take an economy trip to London. No, I've never been abroad and don't know anybody there, but that doesn't matter. I like people."

No self-centered person could have such enjoyment of life. Many, in a strange city, would hunger for the assurance that someone felt concern for them. They would long for the telephone to ring, feel lost without familiar companions, and regard going alone to museums, taking walks, and attending strange churches a dreary business. My friend skips past such depressing thoughts. Because she is interested in other people she can communicate with them and enjoy the contact, even if they have no special interest in her. She is not looking for attention, but wakes to each day with the eagerness of a child on a summer morning.

She's unusual and lucky? In a way, but there is wisdom here, too. While she would not have chosen the difficult pattern of her life, she has made of it a bright encouragement to all who meet her.

Looking inward, waiting for attention from others, is like looking down a dark well, but, turning to face the light, we see sunshine on the orchard and ripe fruit on the trees.

Our Father, help us always to face toward the light and to remember that our path may be illumined by thy spirit.

» 7. A Personal Psalm «

Return unto thy rest, O my soul; for the Lord hath dealt bountifully with thee. —Psalm 116:7

"I think we each should have a private, personal psalm to repeat when we need reassurance," my friend told me. "This is particularly helpful at night when we are haunted by worries. As we read the book of Psalms now, we realize how often the writers reinforced their morale by affirming their faith in time of danger and trouble."

The psalmists repeatedly pray to be delivered from, or to triumph over, their enemies. We, too, have enemies, not literally waiting in ambush with spear and arrow, but in the form of fears that swirl through our minds in the darkness and threaten to overwhelm us: fears of the future, of illness, of poverty, of the future of loved ones, of loneliness and inadequacy. To build confidence and faith these ancient singers recounted the mercies of God and affirmed their trust until they could say, "Thou shalt not be afraid for the terror by night" (Ps. 91:5).

We all know something of "the terror by night," but we know, too, from experience, that the prospect looks less terrifying in the sunshine and activity of the morning, particularly after we have slept. How can we attain the serenity that leads to restful sleep? My friend believes it is helpful to make a list of things that are true and comforting, to list them in a definite order so that they may become very familiar. Some psalms begin with the thought, "It is a good thing to give thanks unto the Lord," and then go on to tell why and for what. We might borrow such a verse and then go on to a list of our own affirmations. These would vary with individual experience, but the following might serve as suggestions:

1. I thank thee, God, that I was born to parents who loved me.

2. I thank thee, God, that I have done useful work.

3. I thank thee, God, for the riches of deep human love.

4. I thank thee, God, for the experience of parenthood.

5. I thank thee, God, for the friendships I have cherished.

6. I thank thee, God, for enjoyment of nature.

7. I thank thee, God, for the kindness of those around me in daily living.

8. I thank thee, God, for the inspiration of Jesus and the comfort of thy presence.

We reflect on the experiences that have been the richest and most meaningful in our lives. Even if their active phase is past, even if the children are scattered, the parents long gone, the working days officially ended by retirement, each of these has left values that will stay with us always.

A recital, such as this, in a familiar order, lingering to meditate on one comforting thought or another, reaffirms our belief that we have been, and continue to be, blessed. Furthermore no matter what our changing circumstance, we can borrow for the conclusion of our personal psalm the words of David, "and I will dwell in the house of the Lord for ever."

Our Father, may the good things we have known enrich our present days and turn our hearts to thee.

» 8. Bedrock «

He is the Rock, his work is perfect: . . . a God of truth and without iniquity, just and right is he.

—Deuteronomy 32:4

Throughout our lives we search for things of lasting value, but our perception and point of view may change as we go along.

A Japanese friend went home for a visit and was surprised to find that her father had found a new and absorbing interest in rocks.

"How did this come about?" she asked. "It seems like an odd hobby for you."

"Not at all," he explained. "You see, young men, perhaps in their twenties, like flowering plants. In their thirties they may become more interested in green trees. By the forties they come to appreciate the form of the bare trees, and then as they grow older, they find a satisfying study in rocks."

Perhaps this father's thinking is more Oriental than Western, since many of my gray-haired friends retain their youthful enthusiasm for flowers and trees, but there is a basic reasonableness in his reflection. As length of life becomes uncertain, and the awareness of its brevity more pressing, the mind hungers for elements of permanence. There is re-assurance in the hardness and great age of rocks, for these do not have the limitation of the flower's swift withering.

In the Old Testament God is frequently compared to a rock. In the great song of Moses, uttered near the end of his life (Deut. 32), the simile is used repeatedly. From this comes the phrase so familiar in hymn and prayer, "rock of salvation." The psalmist sings, "thou art my rock and my fortress" (Ps. 31:3). Isaiah speaks gratefully of "the shadow of a great rock in a weary land" (Isa. 32:2). Using the Old Testament symbolism, Paul refers to Christ as the Rock (I Cor. 10:4).

A rock was a fixed and permanent point in the sandy desert. It meant shelter from the sun, protection from enemies, and served as a guidepost in an unmarked land.

As we go from youth to age we find that our ideas change on many things. The work we started out to do may not be the one that we find is rightly ours. We lose interest in some activities, preferring others now. We grow apart from early playmates, we enjoy books that we once regarded as formidably boring. In our religion, however, we may find a value that does not change. While our point of view and perceptions may differ from the necessarily simple instruction we had in childhood, a spiritual treasure does not rust or wither.

We hold a rose and know its petals will fall. We hold a fragment of granite and know it will last into the inscrutable future. Here is a fitting symbol of faith. On this the wise man builds his life and his house. Even when the great storms beat upon it, it stands firm because it was founded upon a rock.

Grant, we pray, that in the changing circumstances of our lives we may find unchanging strength in thee.

» 9. Taking a Model «

And he shall be like a tree planted by the rivers of water, that bringeth forth his fruit in his season; his leaf also shall not wither; and whatsoever he doeth shall prosper.
—Psalm 1:3

Children instinctively take models for their attitudes and behavior. It can be a useful practice as we grow older.

I remember a dear friend who came into our church sewing group one morning with a thoughtful expression on her kindly face.

"I've just celebrated my seventieth birthday," she told us, "and I wonder what kind of old lady I'm going to be. I come of a long-lived family and have seen all varieties."

Some of these, she explained, were a joy, and others definitely difficult to live with.

I had the pleasure of being her neighbor for the next fifteen years, and I hope she realized she was just the kind of old lady she hoped to be. She was forever hospitable, interested in world affairs, interested in new members of the community to the point of calling on them and learning the names of their children, loyal to her garden club and church.

37

She enjoyed each grandchild and great-grand-child as an individual, accepted without bitterness the loss of her husband after sixty years together, and met infirmity with courage. We were happy that she was able, just a few days before her death, to entertain and enjoy a meeting of her church circle.

I do not try to portray her as a saintly character, because she had her human failings with the rest of us, but she was intelligently aware of the problems of age and determined to live the length of her days usefully and with zest.

As children we look up to certain individuals whom we admire and wish to emulate. These may be brothers, sisters, parents, teachers, schoolmates, Scout leaders, athletes, or even movie stars. Later, as we are attracted to some type of work or profession, it may be through the character of an outstanding personality. We marry and hope that our marriage will be as fine as that of some older couple. We have children and try to follow the high standards of parents we admire. When we go to work, someone higher on the ladder furnishes an inspiration. In the many facets of our lives, whether at home, at work, in community activity, we have the example of Christ, who taught us to stress the spirit and to care for others. When we see this Christlike attitude of love in pastor, doctor, or humble lay person, we feel its influence.

Without dwelling on them, it is useful to recognize the less attractive characteristics of age. We do not want to talk too much, or at too great length about former times. We do not want to complain or lament or assume that, because something is different from the past, it is automatically wrong. Such were not the attitudes of the men and women we remember with love and admiration.

The shining spirits of those we would take as our inspiration remained warm and flexible, as they lived their last years with kindness and joy and serenity.

We thank thee for the brave and gracious personalities we have known and pray that we, too, may live out our lives saying yes to life and to thee.

» 10. Partings «

Blessed be God, even the Father of our Lord Jesus Christ, the Father of mercies, and the God of all comfort.

—II Corinthians 1:3

Saying farewell to a son or daughter for an indefinite period can be one of life's most poignant experiences.

In the beautiful musical play, *Fiddler on the Roof*, there is a scene where Tevye, the poor and philosophical father in a Jewish village of old Russia, must bid good-bye to one of his daughters. She is very dear to him, and he thinks of her as a lovely and enchanting child. But now she has fallen in love with a fiery young idealist who has been exiled to Siberia, and she is determined to follow him. Between poverty and the threat of pogroms, life has been a chancy thing in the village, but it has been home and the family ties have been strong. As father and daughter wait at the railroad crossing for the train the girl falters momentarily as she suddenly realizes that perhaps she will never be back there with her people again.

"Papa, God alone knows when we shall see each other again," she murmurs.

Her father, out of the depths of his sorrow, knowing far better than she the dangers of her decision, takes her hand and says gently, "Then we will leave it in his hands."

Often at airports I have seen the sorrow in the eyes of aged parents as they say farewell to their children. The question, "Will we see each other again?" is always there. "Why is it," one of them asked me, "that today our children must scatter to the ends of the earth?"

This is nothing new, although surely more of our children go farther than in previous generations. In the days of heavy immigration the Irish, Italian, Polish, Russian, and Swedish parents who saw their children embarking for a new land had much less chance of seeing them again, or indeed hearing from them. Many did not have the education for writing letters, travel was slow, costly, and hazardous. Today overseas assignments are usually limited and broken with leaves. Airmail letters wing across the sea or continent. It is possible—and how tempting—to talk by long-distance telephone, and we have the comfort of knowing that our children can fly back as fast as they have flown away.

Although we recognize all these things, the poignancy remains at parting, whether children are going off to college, leaving, with a rice-strewn wake, for the new estate of matrimony, taking a distant job, going abroad as a goodwill representative or on a service mission, or facing the harsh realities of the armed forces. We have watched them develop from babies to purposeful young people. We have shared their problems and joys, and their bright young spirits have lighted our homes. They cannot know—and we would not wish it—how much we will miss them, but we can be proud of their courage. We will be in close touch with their doings, regardless of miles. If we are troubled by the dark doubt, "God knows when we will see each other again," Tevye has offered us the true and comforting reply, "Then we will leave it in his hands."

Grant us the faith that even if physical distance separates us from those we love, we can always stay close to them in our prayers.

» 11. Answering Hard Questions «

He shall call upon me, and I will answer him: I will be with him in trouble. —Psalm 91:15

How does one deal with the difficult questions thrown at us by embittered persons, such questions as "Why must I go on living?" "Why did this happen to me?" "What good are churches?" "If God is good, why can this be?"

A minister, making his hospital rounds, noticed a name that was familiar. He knew some of the family but had never met this man who worked in a tavern in a small western village. When he introduced himself to the man, who was seriously ill, the patient looked anything but pleased.

"What good are churches?" he demanded scornfully. "Church members, I see plenty of them on my job, and they're not any better than anyone else. I'm just as good as they are any day. Hypocrites!"

The minister listened calmly to all he had to say and then asked how he felt. As the man gradually became less belligerent, the caller asked if he had ever had any contact with the church.

"Sure. I used to go to Sunday school . . . all the good it did." He thought back for a minute. "Funny thing I just remembered. All the kids had to learn stuff by heart. They all took easy verses, but do you know what I did?"

"What?"

"I learned the whole ninety-first psalm."

"Good for you! Do you remember any of it?"

"Let's see. 'He that dwelleth in the secret place of the most High shall abide . . . err . . .' "

"Under the shadow of the Almighty."

"I will say of the Lord He is my refuge . . .' "

Stumbling over the words, unthought of for years, prompted now and again, he struggled through the entire psalm and then lay back with an air of accomplishment.

"Well, Reverend, I guess churches aren't all bad. You're putting up a new building, aren't you?"

"Yes, we're working on it."

"Tell you what, when I'm better I'll stop by with some money for it. Come again, won't you?"

Money was the last thought in the pastor's mind when he entered that hospital room, but he left with humble gratitude that, once again, a certain spiritual technique had been effective in turning hostile thoughts into happier channels.

Sometimes people lash out with bitter questions

44

in an almost childlike bid for sympathy. To some of these questions only God holds the answer, but when a sufferer reaches out his hand for help, we grasp it as best we can. We hear him out without debate and, when the storm subsides, we respond with other questions: You have had a rich life. What has given you the most satisfaction? What is the secret of those beautiful begonias you grow? What are your favorite books? What is that fine son of yours doing now? What about your church has meant the most to you?

No two people may respond to the same question, and finding the right one calls for experiment and intuition. Long before the days of modern psychology Paul understood the importance of rechanneling thought. Listing the good and the beautiful, he admonished, "Think on these things" (Phil. 4:8).

Sharpen our intuition, we pray, that we may see the hurt behind bitterness and speak helpfully to another's need.

» 12. Renewal «

The Lord shall bless thee. . . . Yea, thou shalt see thy children's children, and peace upon Israel.

—Psalm 128:5, 6

When we are young the prospect of becoming grandparents seems both remote and formidable. Grandparents we regard as venerable old people. When the time comes, we do not feel old at all, but we feel full of wonder. A friend, whose daughter had just become the mother of a little son, put it very well, "Why, when I saw that baby it was just like falling in love all over again!"

It is a moving experience to see for the first time the tiny child of our child. One feels a welling up of tenderness and a sense of renewal. There is continuity here and, as though our eyes had just been opened, we are struck with the simple truth we have always known in theory, that our lives are a single link in the long chain of mankind.

As time goes by and other children come, the first wonder may be misted over by the familiar and natural pattern of young families: noise, incessant activity, runny noses, tears over broken toys, spinach eaten by hand, bruises. But there are also little off-key songs, sudden kisses, and the lovely feeling of a small hand slipping into a big one. There is the big adventure for a small guest in spending the night away from home. There is man-to-man talk, ignoring the gap of two generations, when grandfather gets down on the floor to consult on a building problem. Many of our fellow grandparents enjoy entertaining one of a family of children at a time. This is less taxing and sends the child, singled out for his turn of special attention, home in a happy glow of benevolence which benefits the whole family.

Keeping in touch with children benefits the grandparents as well. With them they can indulge in fantasy. They laugh more often. They are more active. They share a fresh view of clouds and flowers and grasshoppers, an eager interest they have almost forgotten. They can tell stories, read books aloud, answer questions and discuss God and Jesus at any hour of the day, even if it isn't Sunday.

Not everyone who loves children is fortunate enough to be a grandparent, but, if there are young families nearby, the neighbors' children may enjoy a sympathetic listener. Many of the best-loved baby-sitters are older women who find joy and satisfaction in mothering.

An interesting foster grandparent program is being tried out in many cities by the U.S. Department of Health, Education, and Welfare. This will serve the double purpose of augmenting income and of letting the "grandparent" establish a one-to-one relationship with a child in a hospital, institution, or foster home, through a regular schedule of visiting or care. Babies, for instance, need more than feeding and physical care, but overburdened nurses do not have time to play with and cuddle them. There are many foundlings, crippled children, children with no strong family ties, and those with emotional problems. Understanding persons can help these thrive.

Grandchildren are surely one of the sweetest rewards of maturity. What more precious compliment could one receive than the shy, sincere words, "I like you, Grandma," or "You're nice, Grandpa." Here, indeed, is renewal.

Our Father, we thank thee that, after our own children are grown, we may once again know the wonder of new lives. May we love them with wise understanding of their needs.

» 13. Keep Learning «

A wise man will hear, and will increase learning; and a man of understanding shall attain unto wise counsels.

—Proverbs 1:5

Are we too old to learn? If we are tempted to think it is no longer worth the effort, we might consider the thoughts of Supreme Court Justice Oliver Wendell Holmes. In an address on his ninetieth birthday, he said:

The riders in a race do not stop short when they reach the goal. There is a little finishing canter before coming to a standstill. There is time to hear the kind voices of friends and to say to one's self, "The work is done." But, just as one says that, the answer comes: "The race is over, but the work never is done while the power to work remains."

At the age of ninety-one he resigned. Having all the pressure gone seemed strange and unnatural. He tried idling, but, after a lifetime of intense activity, including being wounded in three battles of the Civil War and fighting many more battles for human rights in the courtroom, he could not let his mind become lazy. He called for his secretary to begin a program of reading from the great books of the past. One day, soon after his inauguration, President Franklin D. Roosevelt came to call and found the learned justice reading Plato.

"Why do you read Plato, Mr. Justice?"

"To improve my mind, Mr. President."

In the words of Catherine Drinker Bowen, author of the fine biography, *Yankee from Olympus:*

"To the beholder there was something enormously reassuring in the spectacle of a man so old and so wise, who still desired to learn."

Each reflecting person knows some mind and voice that speak to him through books with special meaning. For the religious person the collected writings in the Bible hold fathomless significance. Here may be found ever-new refreshment as in the clear waters of a spring. The diverse books of the Bible speak with different voices and meet response in different people. Some readers may prefer Luke or John, some find the greatest depth in the writings of Paul. Others, conceding the value of the New Testament for its revelation of the life of Christ, are inspired by the music of the Psalms, the poetry of Isaiah, the majestic dilemma of Job, or the shrewd wisdom of Proverbs.

There is more than one way of reading the Bible. We can go back over our favorite passages until they become as familiar as the sidewalk leading to our house. Or we can try to understand them better by also reading about them. Reading with a commentary gives a new dimension to some chapters. Some modern novels on biblical themes, even if the action is occasionally imaginary and off-key, can give the color and feel and life of the times. Many people have found inspiration and new understanding through the books of Mary Ellen Chase on the Bible, the Psalms, and the prophets, all written for "the common reader."

It is easy to slip into a routine of reading only the daily paper and, perhaps, a weekly magazine. We can stretch and deepen our minds by going back to the rich sources.

Help us to look for meanings and to learn from the great souls who have found eternal truths.

» 14. Heritage «

Yea, I have a goodly heritage. —Psalm 16:6

How little we know of the lives of our forebears!
We can trace lines of descent on a chart, but the
names scarcely become people unless we have letters
or diaries, or unless we have heard stories about
them. Often we treasure these stories as glimpses
into the past.

My father was the youngest child of a clergyman
of the "Middle Border." While these were not
pioneer times, life was still simple and hard. My
grandfather had a farm to feed his family and sup-
plement his meager earnings from the church, but
he was a bookish man and farming was simply a
necessary struggle for survival. One year the harvest
was poor and my grandmother became seriously ill.
The boy was told that there could be no Christmas
that year. Children did not expect lavish gifts in
those far-off days, but the child felt desolate.

On Christmas day he encountered his best friend
who called out cheerily, "What did you get for
Christmas?"

With a lump in his throat, he shook his head.
"Nothing."

His friend looked at him with surprise and real concern. Nothing! That was awful!

He thought a moment then reached in his pocket. "Look. I've got two knives. You take this one."

This made all the difference! Now my father had a present, an almost brand new pocketknife of his own. It was a present he remembered all his life. He told his children about it. I told my children and my grandchildren.

Each of us has lived a life that is unique and not quite like any other. We have heard tales of our parents' early years, and talk of our grandparents, aunts and uncles, but the days of "Dear Diary" are over. Letter writing has become sketchy, as it is so much easier to reach for the telephone, but telephone conversations leave no trail. What we know will vanish with us unless we leave some written record. Most of us have the experience at some time of wanting to know something about an early member of the family, a name, a place, "Whatever happened to him?" We say ruefully, "Why didn't I ask my grandmother or uncle? No one knows now."

It does not take literary skill to jot down names, dates, early recollections of family life, personal experiences and the qualities that characterized members of our families. These things reach back beyond the ken of our children. In such a record we could pass on stories of faith and courage, sacrifice and achievement. If writing is difficult it is easy to talk with a tape recorder. It is easy, too, to write names on the backs of family photographs.

People read with interest the memoir written by Lyndon B. Johnson's mother, telling of her early years, his birth and childhood. While we may not be the parents of presidents, we, too, have things to tell. Just recently my own son, from across the continent, said, "We know so little about your life. Why not write it down?"

Looking back, we see we have a "goodly heritage." With the leisure of our later years we have a beautiful opportunity to pass it on.

We thank thee for those who have made our heritage possible. May we keep their memory alive to deepen the understanding of other generations.

» 15. What Have I to Give? «

Such as I have give I thee. —Acts 3:6

One of the joys of life is giving. Even when people are in the position of Peter who said, "Silver and gold have I none," they can also say with him, "but such as I have give I thee." We can give of our life-long accumulation of experience and understanding.

"I make buttonholes," a woman in a church sewing group told me. "I have made thousands of them on the garments we send to needy people. Not everybody likes this job, but this is my specialty. . . . Sometimes, when there is a lull in the work I even get lonesome for buttonholes." This is her special skill, and she uses it as a service to the Lord.

Another woman, in a county home, had always loved music with no opportunity for instruction. There was a piano in the home with no one to play it. She heard about a correspondence course and sent away for it. From what she painstakingly learned of musical notation, combined with a good natural ear for music, she began picking out the melodies on the keyboard and soon was able to play simple accompaniments. It wasn't proper playing, but it gave the other residents great pleasure to gather around the piano in the evening and sing familiar songs and hymns.

An old gentleman, living alone, had received many kindnesses from friends and neighbors. He could not buy them gifts and would not know what to buy, but his black walnut tree had yielded a large crop. He harvested it carefully and spent long winter evenings cracking the hard nuts, picking out the meats, and putting them in small Christmas boxes for his friends.

Even when people do have "silver and gold" there is satisfaction in giving that is born of understanding.

The wife of a successful business executive had grown up in an orphanage. She knew, from unhappy experience, how sad it is for children to receive no mail. As her personal project, this woman obtained the names and birthdays of all the boys in a nearby home that cared for youngsters of troubled background. For more than ten years she has sent a birthday card to each boy in the home. The response, in the way of Mother's Day and Valentine greetings, shows that her messages have gone to the heart.

A very wealthy retired industrialist, concerned by the waste of business skills among his fellow retirees, set up a clearinghouse where men and women needing help or advice with small businesses could go for counsel from one of the many experts who have volunteered time and talent.

Some of us have special skills, some are blessed with native talent, some have had extensive training. Some, with no formal training, have the gift of understanding, the willingness to listen, the talent to say the right word of encouragement at the right time.

What have we to give in our later years? There is no answer in the back of the book, but as Peter, in the name of Jesus, could give healing, so we, in Jesus' name, can give the best of ourselves.

Guide us, we pray, into the path of creative giving and living.

» 16. Discipline «

I can do all things through Christ which strengtheneth me.
—Philippians 4:13

"When my father was an elderly man," a friend reflected, "we used to tease him a little about his rigid daily schedule. It amused us to see him eat certain things at certain times, take naps, read, go for walks, all strictly on schedule. Why, we wondered, when he had so much time, was he so particular about this routine? Now that I'm older, I understand better and admire him for it. Self-discipline isn't easy, especially when there is not much incentive. I know now it takes a lot of character."

We all remember how it is with children who have had too much vacation. It becomes harder and harder for them to do their small chores. Making beds or straightening their rooms can go on for embattled hours. Going on errands or doing their practicing become issues as they grow lazy and indifferent, but when school, or some other routine, reenters their lives, the whole tone changes.

In later life, too, discipline makes the difference between living passively and actively. It is easy to drift, to nod over prolonged reading of the morning paper, to stretch small activities into undue lengths, to watch television in near comatose fashion.

One day I sat beside a charming and interesting woman at a luncheon. I had no idea she was a semi-invalid until some chance remark revealed that her activities were limited. She loved reading but had to be careful not to overstrain her eyes. However, at the start of each week she studied the television and radio programs, noted the ones that she wanted to hear, and put a schedule on her calendar. She listened actively, to learn, to enjoy, and to think. This plan made the difference between using these resources as a soporific or a stimulus. It was a form of discipline.

I know a man who learned that he should reduce his weight considerably. He figured out a practical quota of daily intake and simply accepted this as a new program. He was as tempted as anyone else by the extra piece of coffee cake, the ice cream on the pie, but, perhaps because he was a scientist accustomed to taking a long view, he could see that these seemingly trivial exceptions were really obstructions to the long-range plan. The momentary enjoyment was not as important as reaching the goal.

We all know how tempting it is to take that extra

helping, or to skip our exercises, or to postpone writing that letter or making that call. Small things can add up to a way of life. We remember the nursery rhyme that begins, "For want of a nail the shoe was lost," and goes on to the dire consequence of the kingdom lost. One nail can be important!

If discipline can strengthen our physical and mental well-being, it can also deepen our spiritual lives. In cloistered orders men and women follow a strenuous schedule of service, study, and devotion. They do not do these things when they happen to feel like it, but as the firm framework of their days. We can learn from these and other dedicated people.

Do we have a plan for our days through which we can serve, grow in mind, in health, and in spirit? Each morning that dawns offers a new opportunity for affirmative living.

Help us to live our lives with purpose, turning to thee for guidance and for help in our self-discipline.

» 17. Going on Alone «

Is it nothing to you, all ye that pass by? behold and see if there be any sorrow like unto my sorrow.

—Lamentations 1:12

"Is there any sorrow like my sorrow?" So cries the heart in the pain of separation from one whose life has been interwoven joyously with another's. How does one go on? It is not easy, particularly when a devoted wife has made the home bright and comfortable, and a protective husband has solved the problems and carried the responsibilities. There is no one way, but each must find his own.

Drastic change is the solution for some, as in the case of the widow whose husband died after many happy years together.

"Nothing will ever be the same again," she concluded. "I lived one life before we were married, a second with him, and now I must start a third." She disposed of the art objects they had collected, broke up their home, and left for a distant city, planning to resume a type of work she had done years earlier, and start anew.

Such cutting of ties is not practical for those with children or other dependents. For these, often the wise course is to reenter the mainstream of life promptly. I remember a holiday season when a man of our community met tragic, accidental death, leaving a wife and school-age children. The funeral was held the Saturday before Christmas. The next evening, when we entered the church for the candlelight carol service, we saw, in the back pew, the entire family. It would have been easier to stay away from an occasion of such happy associations, but this was typical of the courage with which this family said Yes to life.

Sometimes it takes longer. Another widow could think only of her grief and wanted to live in the past, cling to her old home, and change nothing. Her friends, full of sympathy at first, became tired of her helplessness, but they stood by and tried not to give advice. Finally she made the painful decision to move to an apartment where there would be fewer problems. Her friends were pleased because they recognized this as a turning point in taking control of the direction of her own life.

An aged minister lived in a church home with his wife, who was failing rapidly. One night, at a service, the husband, with his wife beside him in a wheelchair, offered a moving and beautiful prayer of thanks for sixty rich years of marriage. This was the last time they could attend together. A few weeks later, he offered another prayer, thanking God for his never-failing care and for his love expressed through the kindness of friends.

Here was not bitterness for a loss, but gratitude for a life.

And what of those mentioned so brokenly in the verse, "Is it nothing to you, all ye that pass by?" Not all pass by.

A man plunged in grief by the sudden loss of his wife was visited by men he had known for years. "You need a fire," they said, started a great crackling blaze and left him with a pile of wood stacked high beside the fireplace. It was a simple but never forgotten act, symbolic of the role of friends.

Those who say Yes to life do not deny or gloss over the depth or intensity of the sorrows that are integral parts of human experience. Strengthened by love, they acknowledge that, although one life has ended, another remains to be lived.

Grant us the faith to accept sorrow, but reject despair, to face life bravely enriched by the love we have known.

» 18. I Believe «

While ye have light, believe in the light, that ye may be the children of light.

—John 12:36

Do we ever stop to figure out exactly what things we believe? It is an interesting and revealing exercise.

One man who did was John Bartram, who built, with his own hands, a sturdy stone house on the banks of the Schuylkill River in the year 1730. The house, surrounded by beautiful old trees, now belongs to the park system of Philadelphia, fortunately rescued from the tide of industrial plants with giant smokestacks that loom beyond the trees. Bartram was a self-taught pioneer in the field of botany, a farmer, who became a giant in the estimation of European scholars and scientists. Honors came to him. Great men visited his famous garden and the house where he lived simply, and where his Negro servants dined with the family.

A member of the Society of Friends, John Bartram was a godly man—but did not always see eye to eye on religious matters. According to tradition he was "disowned" by the Meeting for his views.

He was not bitter about this, but put his hat squarely on his head and joined his neighbors regularly for worship at the meetinghouse. Some forty years later he incorporated his long-held creed into a few lines carved on a stone in the wall of his house. It is still there for visitors to ponder,

'Tis God alone, Almyty Lord
The Holy one, by me adored.
John Bartram, 1770

It would be interesting if men displayed their creeds for all to see. Not everyone would be certain enough to record his on stone. Many would have a question mark, but each of us has certain beliefs which hold special inspiration and vitality.

In church we repeat in unison the creed of our denomination, rarely pausing to consider the years of study, of searching, of argument, of conference, and of prayer, that lie in back of each phrase that comes so easily to our lips. Creeds are revised, at long intervals, and the painstaking process is repeated to make the words more meaningful to men of the day. Some portions may hold more meaning for one person, some for another.

We have our favorite passages and teachings in

the New Testament, and these usually present things we believe deeply. Among my own are those glowing words from I John 4:16, "He that dwelleth in love dwelleth in God, and God in him." For another, key verses might be, "Love thy neighbor as thyself," "I am the Resurrection and the Life," "Not to be ministered unto, but to minister."

We do not blazon our beliefs, nor carve them on our houses in today's world, and yet they can be evident in attitude, warmth, serenity, concern, and spirituality. They show in the faces of men and women who have lived their religion. Without knowing the details we sense affirmation and seem to hear the words,

"Credo—I believe."

Help us, our Father, to think deeply on our beliefs, and to live what we believe.

» 19. In Happy Memory «

Blessed are they that mourn: for they shall be comforted.
—Matthew 5:4

I sat down to rest after a long walk in Kew Gardens, enjoying the watercolor beauty of an English spring. In the shade of a tree which bore a sign, warning marauders against "bird-nesting," I looked out across a rolling lawn to the swaying, light green treetops. On my bench I noticed a plaque and read the words,

"In Happy Memory of ———— ———"

"In happy memory," what a beautiful phrase! I saw it on other benches and encountered it elsewhere in England and Scotland. Unfamiliar to American ears, this was an expression we might well borrow.

While I did not know the man honored by my memorial bench, I knew that his friends were grateful for his life and felt that this modest honor would be in keeping with his interests and character. I began thinking about the subject of honoring those we have lost.

For most of us the day of the village churchyard, where the resting place of our families adds sacredness to our place of worship, has gone. We move too often. Cemeteries on the fringes of cities are neither easy nor appealing to visit. The stone monument is no longer as important to us as finding some special way to honor the spirit and contributions of those we love.

In Victorian days mourning was stressed. Paintings or needlework pictures with motifs of weeping willows and weeping relatives were popular for wall decoration. Grief in bereavement is deep and human and natural. There is a time for grief, and its expression is important for the healing process. But there is a time, too, to transcend the thought of death. Who would wish to be remembered in his time of illness and extremity? Is it not a greater honor to remember a loved one at his best, in the full flower of life?

In the Russian novel, *The Brothers Karamazov,* we read of a saintly old monk comforting a heartbroken mother.

"It is Rachel of old, weeping for her children . . . . A long while yet will you keep that great mother's grief. But it will turn in the end into quiet joy."

The dark hour of the Crucifixion is not to be forgotten, but Easter, the great day of the Christian

for words of approval. The skillful teacher finds much to praise, even if the achievement is as small as a neat paper. The child grows with encouragement. Not only in childhood, but all our lives we prize the approval and affection of those whom we hold in high regard.

Among the most poignant words of the New Testament are those recorded of the baptism of Jesus, "This is my beloved Son, in whom I am well pleased" (Matt. 3:17). Too sacred to be borrowed for our own families, these words express the crowning joy of all parents, a joy that can be conveyed in our own diverse ways.

There are other relationships beside that of parent and child where we often intend to express appreciation and do not always get around to it. One of the rewards of the ministry is the letter, or the spoken word of thanks, perhaps years later, for comfort or guidance. The teacher treasures the letter from a grateful parent whose child has been helped to develop. Do we remember to thank those friends who have rejoiced and grieved with us for their sustaining love? The doctor values the letter of thanks for his care from one who has recovered, and words of appreciation for his efforts in behalf of a patient who could not recover.

There are many opportunities in our everyday relationships, such as praise for the newsboy whose deliveries are prompt. There are benefactors whom we do not know personally but wish to thank. I have always regretted that I did not carry out my plan to write a letter of thanks to John D. Rockefeller, Jr., for the Cloisters, sections of the Palisades, and other magnificent gifts enjoyed by the citizens of New York. I knew just what I was going to say, but I picked up the paper one morning to learn that he was gone.

If we cultivate the habit of speaking from the heart as we go along, we will always have the satisfaction of knowing that the things we wanted to say have been said.

Our Father, we thank thee for the kindnesses we have enjoyed from so many sources. Make us quick to thank, that we may enrich and encourage those around us.

» 21. As Whole as Possible «

Wilt thou be made whole? —John 5:6

One Sunday morning, in my childhood, I listened to a sermon on the text, "Wilt thou be made whole?" It seemed a foolish question, since, naturally, anyone who was sick would be willing to take medicine, or any treatment, to get up and be able to do interesting things again. I know now that this is no foolish question, but one that is basic and important. In the later years, when we know we will never enjoy the vitality of youth again, we might ask if we are willing to make the effort to be as whole as possible. We all know people who have given up.

She looked wistful, felt left out, but she wouldn't wear a hearing aid. He wanted to visit the new museum but couldn't face the humiliation of a wheel chair. She wanted to look attractive but wouldn't keep to a diet important for health as well as weight. People thought she was unfriendly, but she didn't like to wear glasses and faces were blurred. The stroke had made speech difficult, but why, at his age, should he struggle to learn like a child? She had trouble eating but wouldn't face the dentist.

Some older people with handicaps are not to

blame for being resigned to them. A survey made by the Community Service Society in New York City revealed that many older people, particularly those with less education, assumed that illness and impairment were simply to be expected with age and there was no use trying to do anything about it. Today much can be done to alleviate physical handicaps and more help, both medical and financial, is available than ever before. It still takes effort, however. It may mean many inquiries, long, tiresome hours in doctors' waiting rooms, temporary discomfort of treatment or surgery, a worrisome interval of getting used to a new hearing aid, glasses, or walking aid, but it results in living more fully. Former activities can be renewed, new interests pursued, and freer contact established with other people.

Not all the handicaps are physical. The incentive to struggle to walk again after, for instance, a broken hip may be gone because of financial worry, resentment against relatives, an unhappy living situation. For a long time people thought of counseling as guidance for young people or a way to save marriages. Now it is becoming a valued service to older people. Often a pastor can help, or can suggest the right person to consult. In many towns there are councils of social agencies. An inquiry may locate an experienced adviser.

A woman who, all her friends knew, suffered constant pain decided to go along with them on a cruise. How could she, they asked, and she told them, "I'll have this pain wherever I am, but I won't think about it so much if I'm enjoying your company and the lovely scenery."

Life holds more for the people who, instead of sighing, "Why struggle?" say, "I'm going to do everything I can." Their activities and interests broaden, their outlook can be both a pleasure and an inspiration to their friends. Often, after a difficult step has been taken, a person wonders why he waited so long.

Saying Yes to life means being just as whole as possible.

Our Father, help us to face our problems with courage and the will to live our lives fully and usefully.

» 22. "You Have to Adapt" «

I have learned, in whatsoever state I am, therewith to be content. —Philippians 4:11

Is it possible to live a full, contented life in such a place as a home for the incurably ill? It depends on the person. One who can answer Yes to this question is a slight, gray-haired woman, a former teacher, who is currently editor of a weekly *Gazette*, circulated to the guests at the home. She is unmarried, with a lifetime of struggle and hard work behind her, no family, no glowing outlook for the future, but she is living usefully and cheerfully. Perhaps this is why so many of the others, several in wheel chairs, like to gather in her room each evening.

"A lot of women can't believe it when I say I *like* it here. They resent being old and sick and away from familiar surroundings and having to turn over most of their property to the home. They're so negative! I gave up my house, too, but here I get the treatment I need. I'm not alone. If my leg aches in the night I ring and the nurse gives me a pill to make me comfortable. Yes, the *Gazette* was my idea. It keeps me busy getting news for it. Besides, there are so many people here who are hungry for a friendly visit."

The mimeographed news sheet carries such items as "We are happy to see Miss M. up for meals this week" and thought-provoking quotations such as "Life is too short to be little." It is read eagerly and gives news of staff, patients, and coming events.

The editor of this friendly bulletin had to go to work at the age of fourteen, a fulltime job in a bakery. At other times of her life she has worked in industrial plants, cigarette factories, and offices. After a few years at the bakery, her abilities came to the attention of a woman who sent her to a church boarding school. She was a secretary after that but suddenly knew she wanted to teach. It took eight years of night school to achieve her degree and, later, more time for a master's degree in psychology. Guidance was her field—and she could speak from experience.

Today her teacher's intuition helps in understanding the fellow guests. One, a crippled spastic, who had been beaten and neglected in her childhood, wheels herself to the room every night. "I wondered if this girl, whose face and hands jerk, had *ever* had any real affection," remarked the older woman, "so, when she leaves, I kiss her on the forehead and she always says, 'God bless you.'

"I feel sorry for the ones who have been catered to all their lives. It's harder for them. Oh, there are some things I don't like, getting sauerkraut so often, for instance. But I don't get mad or complain. Just push it aside and take an extra piece of bread. After all, to be happy you have to adapt."

Religion helps at this time of life, she believes. Her own philosophy is simple and satisfying: "The important thing is to keep doing things for folks."

Even when one cannot travel far physically, it is still possible for a person of love and understanding, to follow the example of Christ who went about doing good.

We thank thee for the shining spirits of those who transcend their own limitations to strengthen others.

» 23. Adventure by Proxy «

Rejoice with them that do rejoice.   —Romans 12:15

My friend tells me that even when one can no longer travel, it is still possible to enjoy vacation adventure. This year, for the first time, her activities were confined to the church home.

"But I did not feel confined. I felt as though I had several vacations. Let me tell you how."

Usually at this time of year she journeyed back for a visit in the state where she had lived. As this was impossible, she taped on the wall of her room a picture of the state capitol, and beside it a picture of the state house with red roses climbing over the guard rail by the Mississippi. These suggested many pleasant associations. All around were the postcards from vacationing friends, bringing loving messages. She could imagine herself in sun-drenched Mexico, in dusty, vast Texas, enjoying the trip with friends. There were cards from Europe. One of her favorites was from the Holy Land. How amused she was to think of today's shepherds, still dressed in the style of biblical illustrations but carrying transistor radios in the folds of their tunics!

We have all heard of armchair travel, but it is

more enjoyable to pursue it in the company, even if vicariously, of good friends.

Her wall is as gay as a travel bureau with pictures from so many parts of the world. Each card serves as a takeoff point for thoughts of people, for reading, for looking up information about far places.

"I wish my friends could see their cards on my wall and realize how much they mean. I imagine myself with them, seeing all the color and beauty and activity. As I think of those friends in faraway, and sometimes dangerous, places, I say a prayer for them, knowing that, wherever they are, God is."

The ability to enjoy another's joy is one we all have to some extent, but it is an enriching quality that can be cultivated and extended. We all experience it at Christmas when we see the light of wonder in little children's eyes. We are moved, often to tears, by the radiance we see on the faces of bride and groom at a wedding. Watch the shining eyes of parents whose children win applause and honors at school! For many this is more thrilling than any achievement of their own.

The friends we love to talk with are those who listen closely to what we tell, whose faces reflect sympathy, awe, curiosity, or amusement, according to the tale. The person who can enter into another's joy adds an extra dimension to his own life. He can rejoice selflessly when someone, not hindered by his own economics or infirmity, has the opportunity to travel or achieve. He will not lack for friends, because all around him are people who are hungry for one who will have the warm empathy to enter into their trials, their hopes, and their joys.

Jesus entered into both the occasions for weeping and the occasions for rejoicing of his fellowmen. In him they found understanding.

Our Father, help us to dwell one in another, knowing that our lives are intertwined in the brotherhood of thy family.

» 24. Senior Helpers «

Bear ye one another's burdens, and so fulfil the law of Christ.   —Galatians 6:2

The telephone rings in a small apartment, and the white-haired woman who lives there alone answers it eagerly.

"Yes, I'm just fine. No, I don't need anything special today . . . and isn't it a lovely day?" After a brief, friendly chat she goes back to the kitchen, happy in the assurance that someone in her church is thinking of her and knowing that a similar call will come the next day.

A car stops in front of another house and a woman goes in to assist the resident on a visit to the doctor's office.

Down the street, the man in the wheelchair welcomes a man visitor who brings him news of city and church affairs and lingers for a discussion of mutual interest.

These are a few of the services offered by a group of church members who call themselves "Senior Helpers." Their purpose is to carry on a mutual aid program as part of the vital life of the church. This is a very large church, located in the sunny south-

82

west where many people go for retirement. When it became apparent that many of the older members had problems, a questionnaire was circulated to determine such needs as employment, transportation, home nursing, housing, housekeeping help, daily phone check, information on retirement or nursing homes, medical, legal, financial, or other counsel. Two columns were provided for checking, one for "help needed" and one for "willing to help." The survey disclosed that many people needed help—but that even more were eager to help, and that many of these volunteers were members of mature years.

In some churches, particularly those in suburban areas, the older members feel that the program is planned primarily for young families, and that they, if not exactly in the way, are not a highly prized segment of the church body. However, churches across the country are beginning to study and undertake programs taking cognizance of the needs and the value of the growing percentage of older members. Often, many of these have no relatives or close younger friends in the community. To them the church is their family. For these a project such as the "Senior Helpers" is doubly valuable. It offers the older members help as they need it, and, just as important, for those who are able, the privilege of rendering useful service.

Another large church group offers an excellent training program for volunteers to visit in nursing homes. The visitors are instructed in helpful techniques by a pastor and by the superintendent of the nursing home. They then undertake regular visits to two patients, with whom they hope to establish helpful person-to-person relationships.

Such actions show that a large church need not be impersonal, but that it can be as much a community of caring as one of the early Christian churches. Ways of life change, but, whether one travels by donkey or by jet, the need for loving concern remains deeply rooted in the human spirit.

We thank thee for new and dedicated ways of showing Christian concern. We pray that the inspiration of those who walk new paths may light the way for others.

» 25. Crossing Age Lines «

Thou wilt shew me the path of life: in thy presence is fulness of joy; at thy right hand there are pleasures for evermore. —Psalm 16:11

What is the diameter of our circle of friendships? Is it narrow or broad? Has it diminished steadily, or has it been replenished?

As we think back over our friends, each of us probably could name one group that was particularly close, often the young couples who started their jobs and were having their children when we did. We admired each other's babies, sympathized and helped with emergencies, shared our recipes, best tea cups, books, and lawn mowers. We had fun together on picnics, cooperative dinners, and New Year's Eve parties. We have kept in touch with some of these people all through the years, and, when we are together, what a joy it is to remember and laugh about those early, hopeful days! We prize our long-time friends, but their number diminishes as we lose them through death or retirement in sunny, but distant, communities.

Probably it is never again quite as easy to make friends as in the years when children are young, every day is teeming with activity, and there is so much to share. People become less casual and more concerned with status as they advance. The easiest path is to associate mainly with people very much like ourselves. We feel at home with them, it takes little effort, and there is a comfortable feeling of security in such a group. It can also be limited or ingrown, because its members are of one age and generally of one social outlook. Because it is contemporary, this group, like our earlier one, tends to disintegrate in the years when we particularly need friends.

One way of widening our circles to include younger people is to participate in groups motivated by a common interest. We spent a summer vacation in a coastal town popular with artists. At any hour of the day, from sunrise to sunset, we might stroll along the harbor and come upon an art class hard at work. Dressed in bizarre sun hats and smocks, they worked intently, oblivious to traffic and the curious pedestrians who peered over their shoulders. The age of these artists might range from seventeen to seventy-nine, but they enjoyed the camaraderie of a shared interest.

I have been a member of writing groups, photography, and gardening groups, and served on civic committees made up of people coming from diverse backgrounds. No one paid any attention to age differences. The emphasis was on learning together and accomplishment in a special field.

A common interest offering opportunity for service and companionship is available at our own churches. Here, if we seek them, are many activities with a single goal. Whether we sew, teach, arrange flowers, make repairs, help in the nursery, study, call on the sick, lead devotions, take on the responsibility of secretary or treasurer for a class or group, we find refreshing companionship with others, regardless of age, who care for the spiritual things that we do.

When we are working with others for a larger purpose, we cross age lines and find a "tie that binds."

We thank thee for the companionship of those friends with whom we have been privileged to walk. Help us to follow in the footsteps of thy Son who made friends among all sorts and conditions of men.

» 26. "Happy Days" «

So teach us to number our days, that we may apply our hearts unto wisdom. —Psalm 90:12

Sometimes when we see a mature person whose life continues to be useful and full of zest we wonder about the philosophy that undergirds it. Why not ask? Usually such people are happy to share the wisdom of their own experience and to discuss the aspects of living which they feel are important.

Such was the case with a relative whom I had not seen for a half century. I remembered him as handsome, distinguished, and apparently interested in everyone, even a shy and insignificant young cousin. I had heard about him indirectly during the intervening years and knew that he had been both successful in business and dedicated to helping others. When a vacation trip took us near his home we had a chance to become reacquainted. Now in his mid-eighties, in spite of a recent, serious illness, he was still handsome, distinguished, and interested in everyone he met.

What had he found to be the secret of happy retirement? Keeping active and useful. He had relinquished his heavy responsibilities in civic and philanthropic work but continues, at a more leisurely pace, to serve on some committees, which take as much time as he cares to give. He has found plenty of opportunity to "lend a hand" by either volunteering or continuing to serve. Besides, it was a great pleasure at last to have enough time to read.

Had his religious ideas changed with the passing of time? Yes, in the sense that there was a change of emphasis. At the turn of the century his contemporaries generally did not question the doctrines and teachings of their churches. It was a time when there were great hopes for the Christian evangelization of the world in a generation. It was a time of easy optimism, an optimism which did not come unscathed through two world wars. Like many others, this life-long churchman gradually thought through his own honest beliefs. These emerged in the form of two great guiding principles, first, dependence on God, and second, the spirit of the life of Christ.

And how important did he regard religion in the later years? On this point he was quite definite. Religion, he believed, is always a challenge and an inspiration. At any age "it is vital to a well-ordered mind and life."

He spoke with affection of my parents and grandparents, recalling the happy world of their youth in a way that offered a rare and precious glimpse into the past.

When the time came to part I was sorry to go. We would be living a continent apart, and we might not come this way again. I groped for the right words, but all the conventional ways of saying farewell seemed inappropriate for a man of his years. I think he understood, because he shook my hand firmly, his blue eyes smiling, and said simply, "Happy Days!"

He could say it sincerely, for his own unselfish "well-ordered mind and life" had brought him—and others—many happy days.

Help us, God, to turn to thee for our strength through all our years, and to try to live always in the spirit of Christ.

» 27. Finding the Day's Highlights «

And thou shalt rejoice in every good thing which the Lord thy God hath given unto thee, and unto thine house.
—Deuteronomy 26:11

Strange how a few words can change our outlook! My friend was telling about a woman we both knew who had had a serious accident.

"She's in a wheelchair now, getting along very well, but, of course, she doesn't have the fun we do in things like marketing."

I had never thought of marketing as fun. It seemed more like a chore, this continuing business of finding a place to park, standing in checkout lines, struggling with heavy bags. Suddenly I realized how much I would be missing if I could no longer visit our modern version of the general store, where, under one roof, one finds beautiful displays of sardines from Portugal, cheese from Denmark, ham from Holland, corned beef from Argentina, pineapple from Hawaii, and the mysterious Major Gray's chutney from India.

In my childhood my mother called the grocer and gave the order for the boy to bring over. This was easy because there was little choice: in winter, potatoes, carrots, turnips, squash, and cabbage. As for meat, the usual question was "What do you have in today?" We never dreamed of such things as frozen Alaska king crab or cereals with freeze-dried strawberries. Today's supermarkets are colorful bazaars, with cheerful music playing and always the chance of encountering friends.

How many things do we enjoy in our daily lives and not realize we enjoy? When the winds of winter assault our houses, we might think back to the drafty, uncertain heating of our early days and appreciate today's comfort in both warmth and hot water supplies. There are many physical things that add pleasure to our days: the smell of fresh coffee in the morning, the newspaper that brings the world to our door, in winter the sunlight giving icicles the sparkle of diamonds, in summer the smell of freshly cut grass, in cities the bronze-gold light of sunset burnishing a thousand windows, the thrill of finding a new blossom on the plant we have raised from a cutting.

There are things with more human meaning that bring warmth to our days: a smile of greeting, the words of a visitor, the sight of a child running to greet her father, the thoughtfulness of a bus driver, the meaningful words of religious inspiration.

Sometimes I have played a game with children at bedtime, asking what three things they liked most that day. While their answers, "a chocolate ice-cream cone, the way kitty purred, and the game we played at recess" would not be ours, it is a good game for us to play, too.

In illness we may not have the "fun" of going to market, but in our own room we can enjoy orchestras, plays, lectures, and great events formerly accessible only to those who could be present in person. As we list the day's highlights, we might include the pleasure of an unexpected letter, the kindness of a doctor, the understanding of a pastor.

The capacity to enjoy need not grow dull with the years, even when activity is limited. Each day has its meaningful moments. These are good things and good to remember.

Help us to see that each day holds something of adventure and loveliness. May we have the vision to see and the will to dwell on the good and the beautiful.

» 28. Our Gift to the King «

This poor widow hath cast more in, than all they which have cast into the treasury: for all they did cast in of their abundance; but she of her want did cast in all that she had.
—Mark 12:43-44

When people have it in their heart to give, even when they have little, they will find a way.

Christmas is a difficult time to be away from home. An elderly resident of a church home found her thoughts turning back constantly to old friends and the house of worship which had meant so much to her through the years. She knew just how it would be, the carol service, the Christmas tree, the social evening, the worship service, for she had always helped bake and serve and decorate and sing. She longed to be a part of the activities, but she was not strong enough to make the trip. She longed to contribute to the building fund, but she had no money to give.

One night, when she was almost asleep, she had an idea. In her mind she saw a gay and special Christmas tree, hung with tiny stockings. In each of these was money for the fund. The next morning she began writing to her old friends. Couldn't there be such a tree? She would make the stockings and would they, please, put the cost of any gifts for her in Christmas stockings on the tree?

After some correspondence her friends agreed, not too enthusiastically at first, because they knew she was lonely and wanted to send her tokens of their affection. She set about making the stockings, and her room was gay with red and green scraps of material. The other residents watched with interest as the tiny stockings piled up. On the night of the Christmas party she would have the joy of thinking of the music, the smell of the greens, the friendliness around the "Building Tree." She would know that she was part of it when the stockings were emptied and the money counted. There would be a big card with the words,

Our Gift to the King

Even if she has persuaded her friends not to send her gifts, they will find other ways of showing their love when the time comes. Meanwhile she has the joy of giving.

Who knows what impact her unselfish interest may have? No one knows the name of the poor widow who cast her two mites into the treasury, and she never dreamed of the value of that small gift. Made immortal through Jesus' words, she has become a symbol of selfless giving. A gift, made with love and sacrifice, can be more precious than its cash value suggests. It has done away with the idea, "There's no use in my giving anything. It would be too small to make any difference." But it does make a difference in two ways. First, many small gifts add up to a large one. Think of the hundreds of thousands of "mite boxes" that have been filled through the years. Second, the example of giving generously inspires others to do the same.

A recent church letter tells me of a women's "Talent Program." Some offer services: baby sitting, hair styling, sewing alterations. Others offer for sale African violets, doll clothes, lemon curd, ginger-apple jam, and one hard worker is reported as "selling marmalade like mad!"

Whatever our talents, we too, can offer our own special gift "for the King."

Make us aware, we pray, of need and opportunity. Help us to give generously and with joy.

» 29. Tale of Two Women «

Rejoicing in hope; patient in tribulation; continuing instant in prayer. —Romans 12:12

Every adult of mature years has experienced tribulation of some, or of many sorts, but there is great diversity in the manner in which people react.

I couldn't help overhearing the conversation of the woman whose chair was next to mine in the beauty parlor. The young operator welcomed her customer, returning after a long vacation, and asked pleasantly, "How have you been?" Unfortunately the woman told her—at length. She had developed shingles and had a terrible time. They tried this and that. She went on and on with the girl making polite responses. Our ways parted, but when we emerged from our respective dryers, the woman had resumed her account and was admonishing the girl, "Now if this ever happens to you, you be sure to do as I say." The tired, petulant voice continued until I left, and, as I went, my thoughts turned to another woman, who had to have a hard-to-face type of surgery. I was concerned about her and telephoned her, sometime after, knowing it would take time to get adjusted.

"How are you getting along after that operation?"

"Fine," she said cheerfully. "I've been busy, and I just don't think about it much. I figure there are more important things to think about."

Although the experience had not been easy, she had accepted it with good grace and now was putting it behind her, concentrating on "more important things," her work, her family, her friends, and her church.

The first woman was outraged that physical illness had interfered with her pleasure, and it became the biggest thing on her horizon. The second accepted hers, with perspective, as a temporary, if unpleasant, interruption, something to be dealt with but not to dwell on.

The person who allows a tribulation to loom so large that other people and concerns are blotted out, may not realize that he, himself, is the loser. Complaining and grumbling at his misfortune may alienate those who would be sympathetic and can depress them, as well. Furthermore, reiterating his woe can retard the process of recovery. His selfishness can be corroding.

One who can "rejoice in hope," while being "patient in tribulation," will find joy in many things.

Every doctor, nurse, pastor, and church visitor can think of afflicted persons who are a pleasure to visit. When the caller comes in, he is not greeted with a long face and list of troubles. There is a smile of welcome, a gracious question relating to the visitor's interests, an eagerness to discuss matters of mutual concern. This is not a Pollyanna attitude of deliberately stressing the bright side and ignoring the other. Rather, it is the pushing back of walls by concern with matters "more important" than one's individual illness.

It is a privilege to know such people, and we all have met some. Their bright spirits are a blessing. After seeing how they, with all their handicaps, can say Yes to life, we go back to our own worlds with fresh courage.

Help us, we pray, in time of trouble, to keep our vision clear, that we may look beyond our own circumstance in loving concern for others.

» 30. Wills Make Ways «

For where your treasure is, there will your heart be also.
— Luke 12:34

He was an old farmer who had worked hard all his life, never traveled more than a few miles, had little schooling, and in spite of his labor could only make a simple living. When he no longer had the strength to work his farm, he realized that he must sell the land to provide for his last years. In a meadow on his farm stood his great treasure, a three-hundred-year-old sugar maple. The farmer was no poet, but to him the tree was a poem and his own name for it was "Old Glory." In earlier days the Indians had camped and held councils under it. He had watched the birds building nests in it, seen it at dawn and sunset, in storm and rainbow.

How could a man sell a farm and keep one tree? Friends heard of his problem and conferred with conservation authorities who worked out a plan. The farm was sold, but an access lane was kept and a piece of land just the size of the circle cast by the tree's shadow in the course of a day. It was a joy to the farmer to go to his rest knowing that, as long as the tree lives—and it could be two more centuries

—the public can admire and marvel at this magnificent sight, which has an appropriate sign below:

O Lord, how glorious are Thy Works.

There is great satisfaction in knowing that things we care about will last beyond our time and that we can help to make this possible. Every college has scholarship funds that enable young people of succeeding generations to become educated because farseeing people have made ongoing gifts. Hospitals have extended facilities for learning and treatment and comfort made possible through the interest of concerned people.

Those who say Yes to life know that life must be lived for others, and each individual dreams of improvements or conditions he would like to help create. These infinitely varied interests might include conservation of natural beauties, family planning, medical missions, help for retarded children, adequate provision for aged pastors and their widows, education for peace, strengthening of the peace-keeping agencies, education for the underprivileged, mental health.

People who work for long-range programs do not expect them to be put into total action within the span of a single life.

On the rocky coast of Scotland blooms a famous garden visited by thousands. A hundred years ago nothing could grow on the windswept headland, but the owner, a young man with a dream, planted a shelterbelt of trees to break the gales. It was twenty years before they had grown enough for him to plant a flower, and now Inverewe is one of the glories of Scotland.

In the same way our legacies of effort and support can help create conditions favorable to the result we seek. Through such outreach a finite life can have an infinite dimension.

We thank thee that the things for which we have worked and struggled and prayed may live beyond us to serve man and to bring our world closer to the way of Christ.

Though our outward man perish, yet the inward man is
renewed day by day. —II Corinthians 4:16

Usually younger people look to those who are older for example and inspiration, but sometimes age is no factor in a radiant proof of the power of faith in meeting what appears as tragedy.

They were an attractive young couple, both of whom had worked hard for their education. Now they had a pleasant home, two fine little sons, and the father had an excellent job as a scientist in industry. They had many friends, were active in their church, and looked forward to a full and happy life.

At the age of about seven the older boy developed strange nervous symptoms, and visits began to many doctors. They concluded, as his condition worsened, that he had a rare disease in which the sheath of the nerve cells slowly and inexorably deteriorates. This was heartbreak enough, but the lowest point came when the second child showed the same unmistakable signs at the same age. Slowly the boys lost the power to move and even to speak. The parents cared for them at home for more than twelve years, until their young lives slipped away.

How could they do this and still present to the world bright faces that gave no indication to strangers of their ordeal? Not through their own love and strength alone. Early in the experience, in the days of their deep anguish, their minister had spoken words that seemed strange at the time.

"It may be," he told them, "that this suffering will work to the glory of God." Just a few simple words, but words that became a golden talisman in the years that followed. They dedicated their sons to God and asked for strength to carry out the trust which had been laid upon them. They knew the sustaining strength which comes from the prayers of others. The mother found the stillness of night a time for her own prayer when she arose to minister in the dark hours.

They found joy in the neighboring teenagers, several of them of another faith, who would come in and sit with the boys, push their wheelchairs, and stay to permit the parents to attend church. They brought fun to the house and expected no payment because they said they had learned so much.

"I learned," said the mother, "that prayers are not always answered on our terms, and that there is more to life than physical well-being. If there couldn't be health, there could be love, God's love, family love, and a love that extends beyond the home." They felt, with humility, that they might be of service if, through their lives, they might witness to the transforming power of their faith.

Today, a beautiful communion table stands in the church chancel, as a memorial to the two boys. Perhaps a greater memorial was expressed by the minister at the second funeral:

"So many of us have come to you wanting to help, ... but you have healed us more than we have healed you. We have been strengthened by the tremendous love which emanates from within your lives. I say this, not to praise you, but to acknowledge that God is using you. What we have seen in you has compelled all of us to grow from faith to faith."

Our Father, we thank thee for the courage of those who can face the shattering of their hopes and find their answer in an ever renewing love. May we learn from them and share in this love.

Charity . . . seeketh not her own, is not easily provoked, . . . rejoiceth in the truth.

—I Corinthians 13:5, 6

"I don't see why people think it's hard to pick out presents," the little girl commented after listening to some adult conversation. "Whatever I get for my mother is always what she wants most."

Her mother obviously had the quality of knowing how to accept with grace, of seeing beyond the little gifts to the love they expressed. This is a quality of increasing value as we grow older, because elderly people are often in the position of receiving.

Just as ministers, who have enjoyed for many years the privilege of the pulpit, find it sometimes trying to be retired to the pew, so active people, who have known the satisfaction of giving, find it difficult to be on the receiving end, whether through infirmity or financial stringency. There may be visitors they do not feel like seeing, clothing they dislike, books not to their taste, flowers that make them sneeze, or transportation in cars that are hard to get into.

There are two ways of dealing with such situations,

and they are both honest. The first is to make critical comments giving a completely candid opinion of the offerings, with a probable bruising of the giver's spirit. The second is to express thanks with a warm and honest appreciation for the thoughtfulness of the giver. With this feeling clearly established, it is often possible to make diplomatic suggestions for the future.

A lesson in consummate tact may be found in the story of James Logan, a young Irishman, who came to this country as William Penn's secretary and lived to be Chief Justice of Pennsylvania. He built a fine home in Germantown where he welcomed both the great men of the day and the Indians, who were free to camp beside the stream that flowed through his grounds. He was held in high esteem by people of all ranks. One day, as a rare tribute, a chief with the unwieldy name of Wingohocking proposed an honor to his friend. They would exchange names. He would become Logan and Logan would become Wingohocking. With quick wit and deep understanding, the Irishman welcomed the chief to the use of the name Logan. For himself, he acknowledged the great compliment, but said, rather than take the chief's name, he would confer it on the stream that flowed past the camp and then, long after he had passed away, and as long as the earth endured, the stream would flow with the name of Wingohocking.

"It is more blessed to give than to receive," and it is often more enjoyable, but it can be blessed to receive as well. Jesus demonstrated this in his response to the sinful woman who brought him her alabaster box of precious ointment.

With children we can see an expansion of the spirit as they offer a gift of which they are proud. They grow when generosity is encouraged. For some people, such as the woman with the precious ointment, there is healing in giving, for others, warmth and pride and self-confidence.

While receiving may not always be easy, we are often giving when, with grace, we allow others to give.

Help us to receive with insight, remembering always that the giver is more important than the gift.

» 33. The Heightened Senses «

*O Lord, how manifold are thy works! in wisdom hast thou
made them all: the earth is full of thy riches.*

—Psalm 104:24

One day my friend, whose hair is gray, but whose
life is crowded with creative activities, spoke
thoughtfully, "Every year the loveliness of spring
and the brilliant colors of fall seem more beautiful.
I don't mean to sound morbid, but I can't help thinking that, well, how many more will I see? I feel I
mustn't be too busy to appreciate all this loveliness.
I must make the most of it."

Here is a different point of view from that of the
melancholy poets, and a good many others, who
lament that the seasons seem to be winging past
faster and faster. While one might say it was natural
for my vigorous friend to enjoy the passing seasons,
since she might reasonably expect to see many more,
it is possible to experience deep joy, even with the
certain knowledge that life will be short.

A writer, Bradford Smith, who learned in his early
fifties that he had only a few months to live, kept a
sort of spiritual journal, which has been published

in pamphlet form under the title, *Dear Gift of Life.* In it he writes of his heightened perceptions.

Each morning is new now. I wake to the inner music of thanks for the dear gift of life and with eager plans for the use of the day. The first sound I hear, whether a flock of chirping birds, or the whispering wind or of traffic with its urgency is dear. The growing light is an omen and a good one. . . . Death opens the door to life renewed and re-experienced as a child experiences it with the dew still on it.

A famous actress, recovering from near fatal surgery, was quoted as saying, "All the colors of the world look brighter to me now. . . . The old world looks better than it ever has before. I hope it will always be that way."

Sometimes after the first cold days of fall, we have a stretch of Indian summer, those drowsy golden days when time seems to stand still as it does in fairy tales. How poignant these days are after the hint of frost! We wish their enchantment could go on forever, but we know it cannot any more than a rose can keep its perfect bloom. Because we know the time is short, we appreciate the lovely bonus. We remember those evenings when we played tag, or hide and seek at dusk with the fireflies beginning to sparkle in the damp grass. Perhaps at no other time of day do children play with such whole-hearted pleasure and intensity. They know that the dusk is coming and that their mothers will soon begin to call.

We too know that our call will come. Now is the time to experience to the full the deep and wonderful experience of the "dear gift of life." The time is past to look for the pot of gold at the foot of the rainbow. Now is the time to enjoy the rainbow.

We thank thee for the privilege of watching the changing seasons, in the hills, beside the sea, in city parks and country meadows. As we thank thee for thy riches visible in the earth, we are grateful, too, for all the unseen riches of the spirit.

» 34. The House with the Friendship Window «

Be kindly affectioned one to another with brotherly love; in honor preferring one another.   —Romans 12:10

Some time ago I visited a very old house in Pennsylvania and noticed an unusual feature of the fireplace. It was a long, high fireplace, with the chimney flue over one end and with space at the other for kindling, perhaps, and cooking pots. On the back wall, at this end, was a small window.

"What an odd place for a window!" I commented.

"This is a very special window," I was told. "It's an old tradition in some places. When there was no fire a lamp or candle could be placed on the sill to guide the traveler on the dark road. When the fire was burning he could see the bright reflections of the flames. This is called a friendship window."

No longer do we need lights to guide the sojourners on lonely country roads, but there are many wayfarers who need warmth and welcome. From this beautiful symbol my thoughts turned to homes I had known with friendship windows: the childless couple with an ever-widening circle of young people whom they love and help and understand; the home where international youth hostelers have been welcomed for years—and are now returning with their young children; the home where the children's "gang" is always welcome and where they know the rules; the home where a gracious elderly lady made a point of showing hospitality to newcomers in an old community; the home of a young family where friends with many children were welcome to stay as long as there was floor space for their sleeping bags; the home that opened its doors to an unknown Ethiopian student for a school year; homes where the solitary, the lone, and the lorn are welcomed and honored.

The friendship window represents more than a physical home where visitors are welcome. It bespeaks an attitude of caring, reaching out, understanding another's need. When we meet a person with this attitude, we sense it quickly and truly as the traveler caught the meaning of the bright window. Sometimes these special people are trained in understanding: the social worker, teacher, pastor, nurse, doctor, or counselor dedicated to human service. There are many others among the rich, the poor, the little educated, and those with higher degrees, who warm our hearts with their simple, Christlike quality of kindness.

Perhaps it would be helpful to take a fresh look at the spiritual house where we live. Does it have a friendship window?

Our Father, help us to be people who care and show this care by reaching out to others. May we transform the light and warmth of our own blessing into a brightening of the road for all who pass our door.

» 35. Saying Yes to Change «

No man . . . having drunk old wine straightway desireth new: for he saith, The old is better. —Luke 5:39

When we take a stand that something old, or the old way of doing things, is best, have we come to this as an honest, thoughtful conclusion, or because we are accustomed to the old?

Friends of ours built a charming home in a scenic location. The city around them changed swiftly, in the next few years, and suddenly they found a large motel under construction across the street. There was also a possibility that their property might be condemned by the city as part of a redevelopment program. Their friends expected a natural reaction of distress and indignation, but they found the couple serene.

"We're not really disturbed," the wife explained. "After all, we had a wonderful time planning the house, and we have enjoyed it for several years. We know we won't live forever."

Although they possessed beautiful furnishings and works of art displayed in surroundings designed for that purpose, these people were philosophical and were interested in the long-range improvement of

115

their city. Theirs was an unusual and thoughtful reaction.

It is often difficult to accept change "straight-way." For example, we, whose ears were tuned to the cadence of the King James Version find it hard to approve "the wind blows where it wills" in place of the accustomed "the wind bloweth where it listeth" (John 3:8), a phrase so beautiful one can see the meadow grasses streaked by a fitful wind. Yet the more accurate translation of the Revised Standard Version opens up meanings in verses that were formerly enigmas. "Their line is gone out through all the earth." (Ps. 19:4.) What does this mean? The newer version replaces *line* with *voice* and now we understand.

A minister calling on some lifelong and elderly members of his church, asked why he had not seen them on Sundays recently.

'We don't like coming much any more," the wife explained. "There are so many new people."

It wasn't really the people she objected to, but the church was different. It had changed from a small country church in a farming community to a large suburban church of city workers, and they felt it was no longer "theirs."

Frequently these days, as the tides of population sweep into and out of an area, it seems wise to expand or replace or relocate a church. This is difficult for those who have tender and sacred associations with the old building. It is a test of selflessness to decide if ties with the past outweigh the needs of others to come.

In national and local issues, in art, music, books, education, and social behavior, as well as in our homes and churches, we are confronted with change. While we may always personally prefer traditional styles, the old house, the King James Version, the old church, we will, if we are truly concerned, say Yes to the changes that serve the greater good.

We thank thee, God, for the good things of the past. Grant us the vision to recognize the changing needs of tomorrow's world.

» 36. "I Made Up My Mind to Like It" «

Thou wilt shew me the path of life: in thy presence is fulness of joy; at thy right hand there are pleasures for evermore.
—Psalm 16:11

Uprootings in the early years usually mean promotions, better living, or greater opportunities. In later life changes often become necessary, unaccompanied by the eager anticipation of youth. However, a resolve to meet the challenge of readjustment graciously makes a great difference.

When her husband died, the widow found that she must give up their large home and decided to move to a small and modest apartment. Her friends were afraid that she might brood, in her loneliness, and feel lost without the open-door hospitality that had distinguished their home for forty years. But these friends underestimated the qualities that had made her a leader, a hostess, and a beloved person. When one came to call in the sunny apartment, she asked, with all the bluntness of a long-time friend,

"How do you really like it here?"

"It's a different life," the woman said thoughtfully. "Nothing can replace those years with my husband, but the kindness of my neighbors has been a revelation. There are several here of about my age, and they try hard to see that I'm not lonely. We often do things together. But there are young families here, too, and I sometimes invite them in, just for the fun of keeping in touch with that side of life. The other day I kept a tiny baby here while the mother went shopping."

The telephone rang. "Pardon me," she said to the caller. "Why yes, I'd love to go, and why not come up here afterward for a cup of coffee?"

"But isn't it a difficult change?" her friend pursued.

"I look at it this way—I've been greatly blessed with opportunities for an interesting life and knowing people I have loved very much. Yes, I do miss my husband, our pattern of life, the old house and garden. I had to dispose of things that had been part of our lives for years, but the really important things are not the ones you can bring in a moving van. I love people. I love reading. I like to work with my hands. My faith is important to me. I've always liked to try new things. I'm sure—and it took a lot of hard thinking—that this is a good place for me to be right now. It's a new adventure in living. But, perhaps the most important thing is that I made up my mind I was going to like it, and I do!"

A man who has specialized in counseling older people finds that one of the familiar problems in readjustment is that people are so often "tied to things." It is a formidable prospect for them to contemplate life away from a home in which they, and perhaps their parents, have always lived. Often they cling to it, at great sacrifice, even if the labor and expense are beyond their strength and means.

The widow who had experienced grief and uprooting, faced ahead with good grace. She did not live in the past, but was appreciative of her rich experience. She was busy finding new friends, new things to learn, new opportunities to help. Because with her whole heart she had determined "to like it," her warm spirit was released to give joy and sympathy to others.

Grant that, in each phase of our lives, we may find new and selfless adventures in living.

» 37. Changing the Focus «

I know both how to be abased, and . . . how to abound.
—Philippians 4:12

In later life it often becomes necessary to change the focus of our interests, much as we adjust the lens of a camera to change the field of vision.

"If you have sung a great deal, I think you will always love singing," a friend told me. "I'm not a soloist any longer. My voice is not good enough for that, but I love to sing in the choir and the choral society."

This is a gracious and successful change of focus. There is no lamenting for the days of youthful successes, but an adjustment to reality, and a happy one, because she is both singing and contributing. Her artistry improves the choir. Many choral groups that present, annually, the great religious oratorios are enriched by former soloists who can merge themselves into the larger group. We all know what a help it is in congregational singing to hear a rich, well-trained voice.

"I used to have a large garden," a sweet-faced woman told me, as we sat together during a horticultural course at one of our great public gardens. "I loved to work at my flowers, planting, digging, dividing, spraying, and all the rest, and I was very proud of the results. Now I don't have the place or the strength for a garden, but I've discovered what wonderful experiences one can have growing indoor plants. What a thrill it was when an orchid bloomed on my windowsill!"

Another classmate was a white-haired man who had also been an enthusiastic gardener. He liked to learn but could enjoy plants without possessing them. After our morning lectures he spent the rest of the day in the greenhouses, as he put it, "visiting his friends." These were plants he had watched set out as seedlings, changing from week to week, and finally coming into magnificent flower.

A woman, who had carried long and heavy responsibility in the women's work of her church, declined another term of office.

"It's time for a change," she explained. "I don't want people saying 'she's done this since the Year One.' There are younger women who have more strength than I have and fresher ideas. I'll always be interested and willing to help, but I've had my turn in office. I'll lead devotions, work on the telephone committee and do odd jobs."

The capacity for enthusiasm, in spite of changing circumstances, shows a selfless ability to say Yes to life. The people who can go from presidency to telephone committee, from soloist to chorus, from private garden to public park, from entertaining in a gracious home to offering a friendly cup of tea in one room, have learned that position and possessions are not as important as the great teaching of Paul:

"I have learned, in whatsoever state I am, therewith to be content" (Phil. 4:11).

Help us, we pray, to adjust to change, with a wholehearted resolve to make meaningful and joyous use of our days.

» 38. Making Our Peace «

Abide with us: for . . . the day is far spent.

—Luke 24:29

She was very old, very wealthy, and very ill. It was obvious to her household that her time had come but she clung desperately to a thin thread of life. When a minister called at the house, her long-time servant whispered, "I think she's afraid to die. Can you help her?"

When he went into the sickroom, she was conscious. He took her hand and asked, "Is something troubling you?"

She looked startled and then began to talk in broken phrases of the past. It was a shabby story of injustice to some members of her family.

"God will forgive you, if you are truly sorry," he comforted her and then prayed that the wrongs could be, in some way, righted.

He went away, wondering if this was the end, but it was not. The woman made one great final effort, sent for her lawyer and her estranged family and did all she could to put things right. The next day she closed her eyes and went to sleep peacefully as a child.

When there is a burden of guilt, death can be frightening to face. While Protestants do not have the comfort of the Roman Catholic confessional, they, too, may need to clean the slates of their consciences, not only to face death, but to face life. Sometimes this is done by taking steps to correct a wrong or injustice in tangible form. Perhaps the error is irreparable and far in the past. Often a sincere prayer of confession and repentance is followed by a sense of divine forgiveness. In other cases the burden seems so heavy that it must be shared with someone who will understand and help.

The experienced pastor is neither surprised nor shocked by the sorry tales brought to his study, for he is familiar with human weakness. As he stands in his pulpit on Sunday morning, looking down at the members of his congregation, he knows things about them that their neighbors in the next pew would never suspect. He knows one who is a secret drinker, one who has broken the law, one who has been unfaithful in marriage, one who has had an illegitimate child. He is glad that these men and women are in the church, for they have needed help in rebuilding their lives. He knows human error, but does not despair of human potential. It is his privilege, as a follower of Christ, to give hope and guidance and faith to the troubled.

Sometimes, if the sense of guilt has become too damaging and corrosive, the pastor may suggest someone to help who has more training and skill in dealing with emotional problems. The approach will be not disapproval, but enlightenment.

We all know the wonderful feeling of relief when some long-dreaded event or ordeal is past. In the same way, when we are freed from an old and nagging worry or guilt, life has fresh meaning, and we can face whatever lies ahead with trust and serenity.

Grant us the comfort of thy forgiveness that we may face life and death with hope and confidence.

» 39. Love a Child «

Inasmuch as ye have done it unto one of the least of these my brethren, ye have done it unto me.

—Matthew 25:40

"I have made many prayers for your family and ours to be happy and everything good." So writes a very special little boy in Viet Nam.

We have delightful grandchildren, whom we love dearly and of whom my husband says, as all proper grandfathers should, "I really do think they are exceptional." We have another whom we have never seen, and perhaps never will. He is a thin, big-eyed boy of ten, ours by adoption through a child-caring plan. We contribute to his support, write to him, send photographs, postcards, and little gifts. Each month we receive the original and translation of a carefully written letter. We know he likes arithmetic in school, is fascinated by American Indians, very curious about his American "siblings" who live out west. He treasures his mail from us so much that when the family's little home burned down he wrote proudly that he had saved everything we had sent. A picture that arrived recently shows a great change from the hungry-looking little boy of three years ago.

Our monthly contribution is stretched a long way by the plan which makes us foster grandparents. Because of it the boy and his brothers can attend school, which his parents never could, and education means hope. Additional rice, medicine, and soap mean better health. Yard goods for clothing mean self-respect to a degree that is hard for us to grasp. When the family goes to their temple they always pray for us. They live in an anguished country, but we hope that our little Vinh, with his loving heart, will come through safely and grow up with some training that will enable him to find more satisfaction in life than his parents, who have subsisted day by day through grueling physical labor.

The organization with which we have dealt— and there are others—tells us that many of their contributors are older people who manage to share pension checks with distant children. Sometimes they are so concerned about the future of the children that they arrange bequests to ensure continuing care and education.

Those who are able like to keep up a lifetime practice of contributing to church and charity and perhaps education of various sorts. We send our check and receive a printed acknowledgment, sometimes an IBM card with holes that give our history. Our gift is a rivulet that flows anonymously into the wider stream and we know it no more, although we have faith in its wise use and know, at least in broad outline, the purposes for which it is used.

When we establish a personal relationship with a child, we give more than money. We think of what will interest him. We make the effort to write regularly. We have an opportunity to reach out in love halfway around the world. To the child, his family, and no one could guess how wide a circle, we represent our country and our faith. From him comes an insight into a place that was only a dot on the map. We learn of a way of life unknown to us before.

The appeal of our organization is "Let some child love you," but for foster grandparents, hungry to keep in touch with the world of childhood, the appeal might well be, "Love a child who needs you."

Help us to cherish the individual in a world of statistics and to reach out generously to hearts hungry for love.

» 40. Difficult Decisions «

Let us not love in word, neither in tongue; but in deed and in truth. —I John 3:18

Sometimes decisions affecting one we love can be difficult. Such was the case with a wife, whose husband, after a long, happy marriage, had become ill. She nursed him devotedly, but, as time went on, her strength began to fail. It was beyond their means to obtain adequate nursing help at home, and she lay awake nights wondering what she should do. She loved her husband for all they had shared and meant to each other, but now he hardly recognized her. There was an institution to which she could send him, but should she?

Finally she went to the pastor who had known them both for many years and asked his counsel. He did not answer her question directly, but began to talk about the cycle of human life.

"There is a plan for our lives," he told her. "There is the beginning, birth, then youth, maturity, and finally age, ending in death. When you were a baby and a little child other people took care of you and gave great thought to your welfare. Perhaps you had an illness, or a condition that required surgery.

It is never easy for parents to take a child to a hospital, but they have the great responsibility of deciding what is the best thing for the child.

"At the opposite end of life a somewhat similar situation can occur. An individual, no matter how able he has been in the prime of life, may be unable to make decisions. You have many things to consider. Would this man, who was such a devoted and solicitous husband, want you to exhaust your own limited strength for him? Will he receive better care in this institution than you can continue to give? With more rest for yourself, can you bring him, on your frequent visits, fresher interests and vitality?

"The decision must be your own, considering yourself, as well as your husband, but always remember that a step like this, taken with thought and prayer, can be an act of love."

Many people are faced with the problem of finding the best possible care for a parent, spouse, or a handicapped member of the family. The pastor had found, in his extensive experience, he went on to explain, that in making such decisions, there were usually three conflicting emotions: love, frustration at being unable to give the needed care and, most torturing, guilt for sending him away. Even if the feelings are not recognized as guilt, there may be unease, irritability, or quick flashes of anger that make life difficult for others. When the health and well-being of the rest of the family are involved, the situation can be complex. Fortunately there are counselors, either pastors or the trained workers in family service organizations, skilled in understanding both the difficulties and possibilities of each individual problem. They are able to help a troubled man or woman decide if the contemplated step may be an act of love.

Today more and more people think ahead to their own futures. The growing number of church homes reflects this concern. These have waiting lists of men and women who choose to spend their latter years with others of their generation and their faith, knowing they will receive kindly and adequate care for their needs. Again, it is a difficult decision to give up more independent living and enter the safe harbor of a church or other retirement home. It may take courage, but, often, in relieving others of later dilemmas, this, too, can be an act of love.

Our Father, guide us, we pray, in our difficult decisions, that all our steps may be taken in love.

» 41. The Lord's Garden «

For as the earth bringeth forth her bud, and as the garden causeth the things that are sown in it to spring forth; so the Lord God will cause righteousness and praise to spring forth before all the nations. —Isaiah 61:11

There is joy in doing work we like for a purpose in which we believe. I thought of this the day I called on a man who had an unusual garden. My directory mentioned it briefly as a place where quantities of flowers were raised, but none had ever been sold. They were taken by truck to many hospitals and available to any church. This was called "The Lord's Garden."

As I rang the doorbell, I saw a framed verse:

> If no one answers when you ring
> Don't turn and go away.
> Just wander through the garden gate
> And view the flowers gay.
> And, as you wander, fancy free
> Among the flowers there,
> Perhaps you'll want to bow your head
> And say a little prayer.

Someone did answer when I rang, a white-haired man with a bright smile of welcome, and with him his cordial wife. They invited me into their pleasant home, and I asked them about the story behind the garden.

The man told me he had been a poor boy and had left grade school for work to help his widowed mother. He had always loved animals, and, when his dog died through the neglect of a heartless "vet," he knew that his own purpose in life was to become a good veterinarian. It took many years of struggle, but he finally achieved his diploma from a fine school and built up a successful practice.

Three times, through illness or accident, he had been close to death and was convinced that God had a purpose in saving him. He had loved gardening with the same tenderness he had for living creatures, and when, after forty years, he finally realized that his practice was too taxing, he decided to retire and raise flowers.

By working slowly he found he could keep going all day long. He did more than plant the seeds and pick the flowers. He experimented, kept records, and did test growing for well-known rose and bulb companies. On certain days of the week he and his wife set pails of cut flowers along the curb to be picked up for hospitals and churches of all denominations. He took particular pleasure in growing plants of interesting texture and fragrance which he and his wife, in person, took to a home for the blind.

A little later, as he stood in the midst of his flowers, the sun shining on his white hair, he told me how often he prayed and how close he felt to God while he worked. In sharing his flowers, he was expressing thanks for the many blessings of his own life.

As we turned to leave and were about to go through the gate, I remembered that on the outside was a sign, "The Lord's Garden." There was another on the inside and this one said simply, "And I Am His Gardener."

Many of us have enjoyed special opportunities and satisfactions. How do we express our gratitude? While few of us, at this point, can do it through actual gardening, each of us can find a way. In a symbolic sense we can ask ourselves the question, "Am I the Lord's gardener?" and hope to answer "Yes."

May we who have enjoyed special blessings show our thanks by opening garden gates for others.

» 42. Just for Fun «

A merry heart doeth good like a medicine: but a broken spirit drieth the bones. —Proverbs 17:22

How do we find refreshment? The ways differ as individuals differ, but doing things we enjoy can change our outlook as pleasantly as a fresh breeze on a humid day.

Some people find their fun in work. A man with gnarled hands sat restlessly in a bus station. He looked at his watch, consulted the schedule, got up, sat down, walked back and forth. He was a vigorous man in his seventies, with the weathered face of one who has worked outdoors. Finally he strode over to the desk and spoke to the manager.

"Look," he said. "I've got hours to wait for my connection, and I'll go crazy just sitting around. I'm a painter and my brushes are right here in my bag. How would you like a job done on this waiting room? It won't cost a cent."

The manager started to laugh and then saw how serious he was.

"We certainly could use some touching up. I'll pay for the paint, if that's what you want to do."

For the next few hours the man worked well and

happily. When the time came for his bus, he put away his brushes, took off his coveralls, and looked at the freshly gleaming walls with satisfaction.

"Sure looks better," he commented and went contentedly on his way. It had been a good day.

His pleasure in his skill is comparable to that of the orchestra members, who, when they finish their concerts, go off together to play just for fun, or the doctor, who, on vacation trips, stops at mission hospitals to lend his services.

For others refreshment comes in a sharp change of pace. The statesman forgets his problems in a detective story. The houswife finds enjoyment with friends at a card table or bowling alley. The office worker gets up early on a weekend morning to go bird watching. Painters and photographers lose all thoughts of themselves and the clock when they concentrate on portraying a flower, a landscape, or a face. Walk through any center where adult classes are conducted in arts, crafts, and special interests and see the absorbed expressions. Many of the students are learning new things and find them exciting.

The day is past when people accepted as truth the adage, "You can't teach an old dog new tricks."

This is a passive, even lazy, point of view. An increasing number of older people are trying things for the first time, flying, going camping with senior groups, or enjoying their first taste of overseas travel with such carefully planned tours as those of the National Association of Retired Persons.

How refreshing it is to laugh with a friend when one has been much alone. As tensions relax, we feel new zest for living. The director of a busy senior center tells me that her happiest visitors are those who enjoy people. Rather than mourning the past or dreading the future, they find endless pleasures in sharing activities and visiting with others.

Through losing ourselves for a time, we find our better selves renewed. Like children after recess, we go back with clearer minds and lighter hearts to our own appointed rounds.

In the ancient wisdom of Proverbs we find that "He that is of a merry heart hath a continual feast," a feast, we might add, that is appreciated by others.

Our Father, help us to remember that joy is a true part of our faith. Guide us, we pray, to the refreshment and companionship that help to make our lives effective.

» 43. New Perspectives «

And God said unto Moses, I AM THAT I AM.
                                    —Exodus 3:14

Sometimes an experience that seems disastrous can lead to a new outlook on life and new understanding. Such was the case with an attractive woman whose life had been full and busy, so busy, in fact, that there was an uneasy sense of never quite keeping up, not accomplishing all the things she wanted to at home, in the church, with her friends, and in the community. "If only I had more time I could do so much better," she would think. One day her world blacked out. She regained consciousness in a hospital with a long convalescence ahead of her. Now there was time, plenty of it, but not yet for action. This was time for thinking, remembering, and re-evaluating.

"What a strange experience," she told me. "I find that an interruption like this can leave one with new perspectives—and it's rather comforting! I think I was trying to be someone I really wasn't and trying to do things beyond my scope. Now I have a lot better idea of the things that are important. As I get my strength back, I'm looking forward to being myself and letting the other people do the things they can do better."

Most of us can look back to our early years and remember our aspirations with a smile. Today's accountant wanted to be a rancher, the plump housewife dreamed of ballet, the grocer wanted to be an opera singer, the contented mother of Little Leaguers wanted to be a movie star. Most of us through changing interests, or plain realism, outgrow our early dreams and find that our true abilities may be quite different.

Some, who accept their own limitations, dream of unrealistic goals for their children or husbands, creating tensions and unhappiness in the family. It takes some adjustment to realize that a son, expected to follow in the family tradition and become a lawyer, will be happier and more successful as a landscape gardener.

Enforced leisure, such as that of a convalescence, gives a time for stocktaking. What is important? What, in the time I have left, do I want to accomplish? It is interesting to make a list of the organizations to which we belong and try to evaluate them. Perhaps the members of the book group have such a good time together there is not much time for books; the writers' group may gradually take the place of writing; the committees and lengthy minutes of the church women's association overshadow its real purpose.

When activities must be limited one might ask three questions: Which offers the deepest satisfaction? What do I want to learn? Where can I be most useful?

The mature person is the one who says Yes to what he is and can do best—and does it with his whole heart. He also accepts others for what they are. It is as frustrating to try to be something beyond us as it is to struggle putting boxes on too high a shelf in the closet. They are likely to come sliding off on our heads.

This does not mean that we should say, "I can't do any better because this is the way I am and there's no use trying." At any age we can learn and improve within our own range. We do not settle for simply being a Christian, but try to be an ever better Christion—however, we do not decide to become saints!

Help us to know what is important and to find the ways in which we may grow, create, and serve.

» 44. Saying Yes to the End of Life «

Man goeth to his long home.   —Ecclesiastes 12:5
In my Father's house are many mansions.   —John 14:2

After many years I can still see the little church, so pitifully shabby, the mourners, so threadbare. The woman they were honoring was one whose life had been harsh and who found little opportunity to develop her fine talents. Speaking to comfort them, the pastor told of the glories of heaven. "The streets," he said earnestly, "are beautiful and the houses, there. . . . oh, those houses, they have all the modern improvements."

A strange description, but moving and meaningful to his listeners. For people living in squalor, a fine house with the comforts of modern heating, plumbing and lighting, elegance in furnishing and landscaping, might easily represent a picture of paradise. We dream of the things we hunger for, freedom, fulfillment, well-being, love, reunion.

What is heaven like? What comes after this life? Three clergymen of long experience, and of different denominations, have told me recently that they notice a change of emphasis in the thinking of their people in regard to death. Their parishioners, they find, have less definite concepts of the "furnishings of heaven" than in previous generations. Perhaps this is due to a society where fewer people know stark want and have less need to compensate for privation. These ministers do not attempt any descriptions of heaven, for, as one explained, "We do not know any more about the next life than anyone else." They can speak, however, with assurance, based on their faith, that God has a loving purpose for man and that Jesus went to a human death, testifying to a divine life.

Many people find comfort in the thought of a future life, accepting the words of Scripture without question. Others, finding logic insufficient, go beyond logic and accept as true something they have glimpsed in personal experience or intuitions they trust without attempting to analyze. And there are others, who have little faith in immortality—but a wistful wish that they did.

"As for man, his days are as grass: as a flower of the field, so he flourisheth. For the wind passeth over it, and it is gone, and the place thereof shall know it no more." (Ps. 103:15-16.) We find this thought repeatedly in the Old Testament, and nowhere more beautifully expressed. But, is it true? The plant does not wither until it has grown a root or cast a seed into the wind to assure another blooming. The acts and influences of a human life can move in widening circles into infinity.

When we have lived, saying Yes to life, in Dag Hammarskjöld's words, "we experience a meaning." We have faith in a pattern and a purpose. Thus we are prepared to say Yes to the end of this life. We go to our long home with faith and trust. We cannot know its furnishings, but we know we will be in the care of the God who has given us life and guidance. What better prayer could we offer at the latter end of life than the one with which so many of us began?

> Now I lay me down to sleep,
> I pray the Lord my soul to keep.
> If I should die before I wake
> I pray the Lord my soul to take.